# It's in the B...

## Take-Home Thematic Units to Promote Literacy

# Table of Contents

**Project Editor:** Allison E. Ward

**Staff Editors:** Cindy K. Daoust, Sherri Lynn Kuntz, Angie Kutzer, Leanne Stratton

**Writers:** Nancy Anderson, Susan A. DeRiso, Linda Morgason

**Copy Editors:** Sylvan Allen, Gina Farago, Karen Brewer Grossman, Karen L. Huffman, Amy Kirtley-Hill, Debbie Shoffner

**Cover Artists:** Nick Greenwood, Clevell Harris, Kimberly Richard

**Art Coordinator:** Rebecca Saunders

**Artists:** Pam Crane, Theresa Lewis Goode, Nick Greenwood, Clevell Harris, Sheila Krill, Clint Moore, Kimberly Richard, Greg D. Rieves, Rebecca Saunders, Barry Slate, Donna K. Teal

**Typesetters:** Lynette Dickerson, Mark Rainey

**President, The Mailbox Book Company™:** Joseph C. Bucci

**Director of Book Planning and Development:** Chris Poindexter

**Book Development Managers:** Stephen Levy, Elizabeth H. Lindsay, Thad McLaurin, Susan Walker

**Curriculum Director:** Karen P. Shelton

**Traffic Manager:** Lisa K. Pitts

**Librarian:** Dorothy C. McKinney

**Editorial and Freelance Management:** Karen A. Brudnak

**Editorial Training:** Irving P. Crump

**Editorial Assistants:** Terrie Head, Hope Rodgers, Jan E. Witcher

## www.themailbox.com

Manufactured in the United States
10 9 8 7 6 5 4 3 2 1

# About This Book

What's the key to early literacy? Plenty of rich language experiences both at school and at home! Multiple and varied experiences with oral language (speaking and listening), familiarity with print, phonemic awareness, vocabulary development, reading comprehension, and writing will help students develop the skills needed to become wholly literate. Homework—an essential bridge between school and home—can provide wonderful additional practice in these language skills, especially when presented in an interesting, exciting manner. As we know, parents can be instrumental in helping develop early literacy skills at home. If you're looking for an excellent supplemental resource that not only provides multiple, varied, skill-building language experiences but also strengthens the crucial home-school connection, it's all right here—*It's in the Bag!*

# How to Use This Book

### What Does This Book Include?

*It's in the Bag!* includes 29 units, each based on a popular kid-appealing theme. Each thematic unit offers

- a suggested list of popular children's picture books
- an organizational chart detailing
  — the significant literacy skills and activities featured
  — the additional materials needed (aside from basic supplies the parent is requested to obtain)
- a selection of reproducible activities and patterns that accompany the highlighted books
- family-oriented extension ideas

You'll also find guidelines to help you manage this program, including tips and checklists for school and home.

### How Do I Get Started?

We've done the planning for you, so assembling each theme-related bag is a snap!

- Choose a theme. Read the introductory page of that unit, paying special attention to the skills featured and materials needed.
- Refer to the suggested booklist or make choices of your own, collect the books, and place them in a special take-home bag.
- Scan the reproducible activities. Decide if you'd prefer to include all the activities or just selected activities based on individual student skill and interest.
- For ease of use, assemble a kit for each activity by placing a copy of the reproducible and the additional materials listed on the chart in a two-gallon resealable plastic bag. Seal the kit; then place it in the bag along with the books.
  - Place a copy of the parent tips (pages 4 and 5) in each bag. Note that there is space available for you to make any special notes.
  - Program and place in the bag the handy contents checklist (page 7) so families know exactly what the bag contains and what must be returned to school.

## What Type of Take-Home Bag Is Best?

There are many kinds of bags to choose from! Handled, paper shopping bags are inexpensive and easy to decorate and carry. Cloth totes and bookbags are sturdy options. Use your imagination—plastic beach bags, thematic knapsacks, and so forth make fun, creative bags. Use this as an additional opportunity to involve parent volunteers by having them donate or create bags for your class.

## How Do I Manage This Program?

- Begin the program by sharing with families the introductory letter (page 6). You may do this by sending it home or inviting families to school for a short introductory session.

- Have family members sign and return the contract at the bottom of page 6 to ensure they will work with the child on each bag, obtain the needed supplies (listed on the contract), and be responsible for each bag and its contents. (You may wish to provide less able families with basic supply packs so that each child can complete the activities as written.)

- At the time of publication, each suggested book was in print. Most can be obtained in paperback form; some are found only in hardback. Books are subject to wear and tear. To help keep costs low, check book club flyers and even make a wish list to let parents and your school's PTA know what titles you'd like.

- Be sure to keep a supply of two-gallon resealable plastic bags to repackage activity kits as needed.

- Use a copy of the record sheet on page 8 to keep track of the bags. Or, if desired, create your own chart to help you and your students keep track of each bag. See the illustrations shown of a pie chart, a bar chart, and a pocket chart to decide what will best fit your organizational style.

- Some bags are seasonal in theme so you'll want to give each child a turn within a limited time frame. You may choose to make multiple bags per unit to accommodate these.

## Who Helps With the Bags?

This is a fantastic program for fostering volunteer help! Consider asking parents, PTA members, and even community members to help you begin and maintain this program. Much of the maintenance does not require a lot of time during the school day, which makes it ideal for working parents to volunteer.

- If desired, get help
  — creating a bag (or set of bags) for each chosen theme
  — checking in returned bags, replenishing materials, and redistributing
  — creating additional activity kits and filing them
  — managing bag checkouts and returns

- Note: Volunteers who do not have a lot of available time may help provide supplies throughout the life of the program.

3

# Parent Tips

## Upfront information:

What is literacy? Literacy includes reading, writing, speaking, and listening. We use our literacy skills every day in reading books, magazines, menus, advertisements, computers, labels—an almost endless list of possibilities! Learning to read is a continuous process that will build a lasting foundation for literacy. Read the tips below to help you as you work with your child.

- Your attitude toward books greatly affects your child's attitude toward reading. When your child sees you reading and sharing good books, he or she is sure to want to join you.
- Readers read what interests them. They read for entertainment and understanding. Allow your child to choose books that appeal to him or her.
- Readers of all ages and ability levels bring their own experiences to the material being read. The more they know, the more they will understand. The more they understand, the more they will know.
- Choose a special place for you and your child to read. Make it well lit and cozy, with few outside distractions. This should be a retreat for you both.
- Read aloud every day. Your child will let you know how long is long enough. Each reading experience will be different.
- Read at a regular time each day. Look at your child's routine and choose an appropriate quiet time, such as before bedtime or after a meal.
- Link the books you're sharing to your child's experiences in school, other books, and his or her daily life.

## Before you start:

- Look over the materials checklist to be certain everything is included in your bag. You will find a selection of books and kits. In each kit you will find reproducible activity pages and any additional materials needed to complete the activity.
- Familiarize yourself with the book selections included in the bag. Most are popular children's picture books; a few are nonfiction. With longer nonfiction and some selected picture books, it may be beneficial to choose only parts of the book at one time.
- Familiarize yourself with the activities. Be sure to read the parent note on each activity. Consider your child's background knowledge about the topic. Tailor each session to your child's interest and ability. Depending on your child's level of involvement, you may work through the entire activity at once or break it into smaller parts. You may also choose to continue with a different activity.

# Let's get started:

- Choose a book together. Before reading with your child, point out the pictures and talk about the action. Decide whether you will read to your child, your child will read to you, or you will take turns reading together. As you read, use the questions *who, what, where, when, why,* and *how* to ask your child about pictures, words, sentences, and paragraphs. After reading, invite your child to retell the story (or parts of the story) to you in his or her own words. Then ask your child if there was a special message in the book.

- If your child loses interest in the book, don't despair! Put it down and do something else for a while. Try rereading the book later, or choose a different story. Don't force reading—above all else, reading should be enjoyable!

- Select an activity. Read the directions with your child. (Many older children may be able to do this independently, while younger children may need your assistance.)

- Work through the activity with your child. Ask lots of questions and encourage your child to do the same. Give plenty of praise and feedback to your child for his or her efforts and accomplishments.

- When an activity involves writing, keep in mind your child's readiness. Many kindergartners are just learning to recognize, read, and write letters or words and are not ready to write sentences and paragraphs alone. Accept your child's writing and encourage him or her to draw pictures to help convey meaning. Your child may also enjoy having you write as he or she talks. This gives you a terrific chance to model writing skills such as matching printed words and spoken words, writing from the left side of the paper, using capital letters, and punctuating sentences. Older children will be able to write more complex words, sentences, and paragraphs.

## When the activities are complete:

- Be sure to proudly display your child's work in a prominent place in your home.

- Was there anything your child wanted to learn more about? Visit the library together to learn more.

- Was there anything that was difficult for your child? Getting feedback like this from your child will help you work on the next bag together.

- Repack the bag using the enclosed checklist as a guide.

- Return the bag to school by the specified date.

Dear Parent,

   Reading is for everyone! I am inviting you to share in your child's learning with this unique literacy-building program. This program, which centers on themed activity bags, is designed to support and improve your child's reading skills. Each bag includes related books, reproducible activities, and special materials.

   I am asking each family to gather a supply of crayons, pencils, scissors, white glue, tape, a hole puncher, and a stapler and staples. It is suggested that you keep these supplies in a special container in your book-sharing area. Your continued participation will enhance the successful growth of your child's reading and this exciting program. By signing the contract below, you are agreeing to work with your child and assure that the materials in each bag are returned to school intact by the date indicated. Thank you for participating in your child's education!
Happy reading!

_____

teacher signature

# Reading—it's in the bag!

Dear Parent,

   Reading success is found in school and at home! By signing this contract, you are agreeing to do the following with your child:
- read the book(s) found in the theme bag
- complete each activity
- return the bag, along with the books and materials indicated, in proper condition by the specified date

_____

parent signature

_____

additional family member signatures

**Bag title:** _____

Dear Parent,

    This checklist is to help you keep track of the contents of this bag. All books are to be returned to school. Read below to learn which activity items need to be returned. Please place a check mark beside each repacked item. Have your child return this bag to school by _____. Thank you for your involvement in your child's education!

**Books enclosed:**

_____

_____

_____

_____

_____

_____

**Books returned:**

☐
☐
☐
☐
☐
☐

**Activity kits enclosed:**

_____

_____

_____

_____

**Materials to be returned:**

_____

_____

_____

_____

**Bookmark**

**Reading is in the Bag!**

# Teacher's Record Sheet

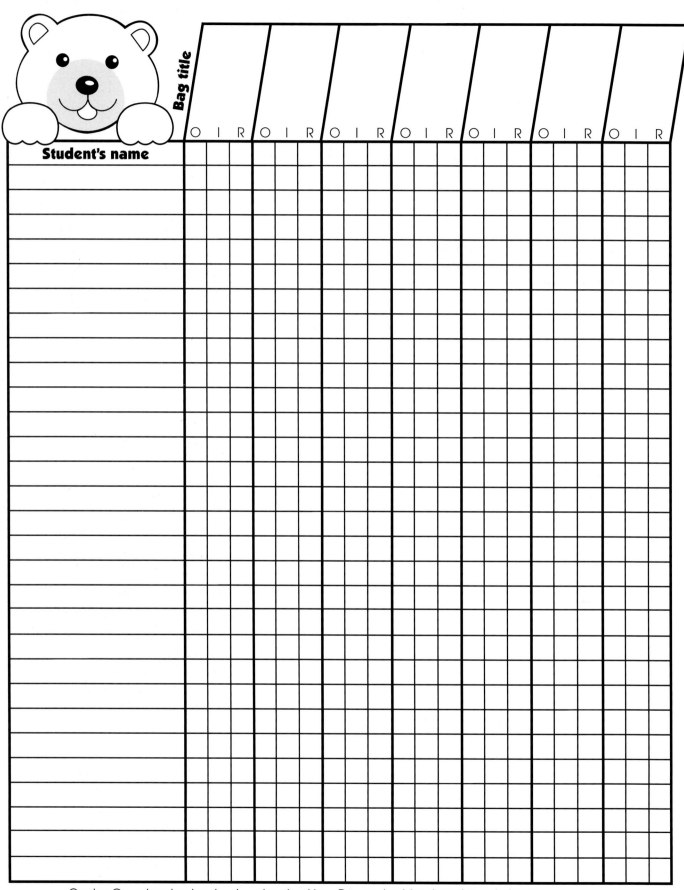

**Bag title**

**Student's name**

| | O | I | R | O | I | R | O | I | R | O | I | R | O | I | R | O | I | R | O | I | R |
|---|---|---|---|---|---|---|---|---|---|---|---|---|---|---|---|---|---|---|---|---|---|

Code: O = checked out   I = checked in   R = replenished and ready to go

©The Education Center, Inc. • *It's in the Bag!* • TEC4100

**Note to the teacher:** Program a copy of this sheet with students' names; then make a supply and program each copy with seven bag titles. Use the sheets to help manage the program.

8

# Apple Mania!

Your youngsters and their families will enjoy biting into these hand-picked apple activities!

## A Book a Day

Pick a bushel of apple books for some healthy family reading. An apple book a day will bring literacy fun their way!

- *The Apple Pie Tree* by Zoe Hall
- *I Am an Apple* by Jean Marzoll
- *Johnny Appleseed* by Steven Kellogg
- *Picking Apples and Pumpkins* by Amy Hutchings
- *The Seasons of Arnold's Apple Tree* by Gail Gibbons
- *Ten Apples Up on Top!* by Theodor LeSieg

## Apple Activities Aplenty

Plant the seeds of learning with these "a-peel-ing" apple activities for students and their families.

| Skill—Activity | Title | Materials |
|---|---|---|
| Oral language—conversation prompts | "Apples and More!" | copy of page 10 |
| Number words—game | "Apple Seed Toss" | copy of page 11, scrap paper, snack-size resealable bag of clean apple seeds |
| Vocabulary—cooking | "Happy 'Apple-y' " | copy of the top of page 12 |
| Oral language—poem | "Happy 'Apple-y' Poem" | copy of the bottom of page 12 |
| Following directions—display | "The Seasons of My Apple Tree" | copy of *The Seasons of Arnold's Apple Tree* by Gail Gibbons, white construction paper copy of page 13, sheet of white construction paper |
| Vocabulary—word find | "An Apple for Today" | copy of page 14 |

### More to Munch On!

- For added interest, enclose a note inviting your little ones and their families to have an apple taste test using red, green, and yellow apples. Have them determine which kind is crunchiest, sweetest, and tangiest.

- Enclose a note encouraging the family to take a trip to a local apple orchard or farmers' market and pick some special apples.

# Apples and More!

**Directions:**

1. Choose an apple.
2. Read it to someone.
3. Talk about what it says.
4. Color the apple.
5. Repeat Steps 1–4 until all the apples are colored.

**Parent note:** If you have an apple, start this activity by slicing it and sharing it with your child. Help your child read and follow the directions at the right to discuss each apple.

Some apples are red. What other things are red?

Apples are in a lot of foods. Which apple food do you like best?

Apples are fruits. What other fruit do you like?

Apples grow on trees. What other things grow on trees?

Where do you get apples? How did the apples get there?

Apples have seeds. What other fruits have seeds?

Some apples are green. What other things are green?

# Apple Seed Toss

**Parent note:** Are number symbols and number words really related? Of course they are! Talk with your child about the connection; then have your child remove the scrap paper and bag of apple seeds from the bag. Help your child read and follow the directions below to play this two-person game.

**Directions:**

1. Color each apple.
2. In turn, toss a seed onto the gameboard.
   If it lands in an empty box, toss it again until it lands on a numbered apple.
3. Read the number word.
   Write the number.
4. After four rounds, add your numbers.
   Use seeds to help.
   The player with the bigger number wins.

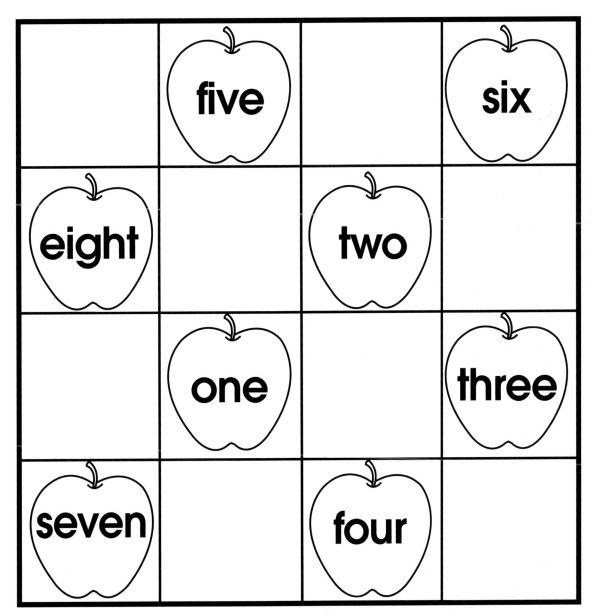

# Happy "Apple-y"

**Parent note:** What's a crunchy, sweet, and healthy snack the whole family can enjoy? An apple! Paying special attention to the boldfaced vocabulary words, help your child read and follow the directions to prepare an apple snack for each family member.

**Ingredients for four Happy "Apple-ys":**
2 apples
8 tbsp. creamy peanut butter
12 raisins
20 miniature marshmallows

**Utensils and supplies:**
knife
tablespoon
napkins

## Directions to make one:

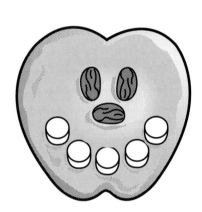

1. Wash an **apple**. Cut it in half lengthwise.
2. Take out the stem and the seeds.
3. Put **peanut** butter on the outside **skin** of an apple half.
4. Add raisins to represent **eyes** and a nose.
5. **Add** marshmallows to make a smile.
6. Eat!

# Happy "Apple-y" Poem

**Parent note:** Review with your child how apples grow; then help him or her read the poem below. For more fun, sing it to the tune of "Twinkle, Twinkle, Little Star."

This is an apple, and it grows on a tree.
It's good to eat, if you ask me.
The seeds are inside, and the stem is on top.
Once I start eating, I just can't stop.
This Happy "Apple-y," all ready for me—
I ate it all, and I'm happy as can be!

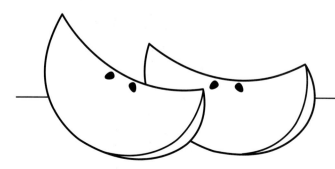

# The Seasons of My Apple Tree

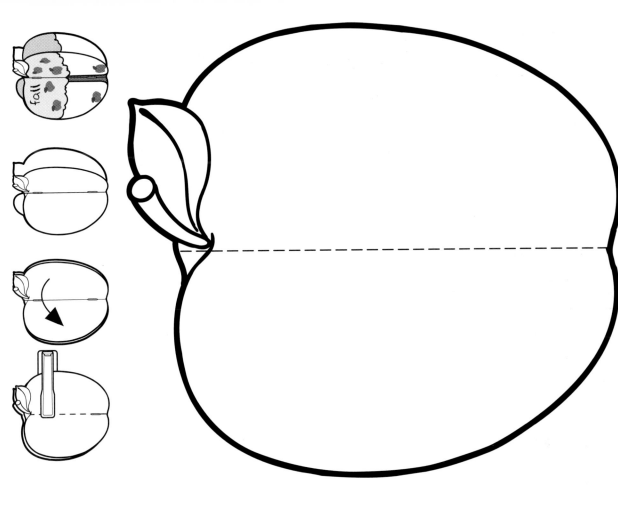

**Parent note:** Read and discuss with your child the enclosed story, *The Seasons of Arnold's Apple Tree*. Have your child remove the blank paper from the bag. To assemble the display, have your child cut out the big apple at the right, trace it onto the blank paper, and then cut it out. Encourage him or her to put the first apple on top of the traced one; then staple them together on the dotted line. Then direct your child to fold the apples on the dotted line and then unfold them to make a standing display. Finally, help your child read and follow the directions below to complete the display. If desired, have your child write to describe the changes in the apple tree each season.

## Directions:

1.  **Spring:** Open the apple to show the dotted line.
    Draw a tree with pink apple flowers and baby leaves.
    Write the word **spring.**

2.  **Summer:** Turn the right page to the next blank apple.
    Draw a tree full of green leaves.
    Write the word **summer.**

3.  **Fall:** Turn the apple over to see the next blank page.
    Draw a tree full of apples and autumn-colored leaves.
    Draw some apples falling to the ground.
    Write the word **fall.**

4.  **Winter:** Turn the right page to the next blank apple.
    Draw a bare tree with no leaves or apples.
    Write the word **winter.**

# An Apple for Today

**Parent note:** There's nothing puzzling about it—apples are good for you! Help your child review the apple vocabulary in the word bank below. Then have him or her find and circle each word in the puzzle. Some words are tricky; encourage your child to look for words hidden across, down, and diagonally.

```
A  P  P  L  E  A  B  C
D  G  R  E  E  N  M  M
Q  O  E  A  G  R  O  W
R  O  S  F  S  T  E  M
E  D  S  X  I  R  C  Y
D  Z  Y  U  M  E  I  E
J  B  R  A  O  E  M  L
K  F  L  O  W  E  R  L
J  U  I  C  E  H  I  O
X  C  R  U  N  C  H  W
```

**Word Bank**

| | |
|---|---|
| stem | green |
| apple | yellow |
| leaf | good |
| tree | crunch |
| flower | juice |
| red | fruit |

# Bears, Bears, Everywhere!

Your little ones will be the "bearers" of great family fun when they take a turn with this activity bag!

## Get Your Paws on These Books

Tuck a selection of these bear-approved books into the bag for some extracuddly reading time.

- *Blueberries for Sal* by Robert McCloskey
- *Brown Bear, Brown Bear, What Do You See?* by Bill Martin Jr.
- *Deep in the Forest* by Brinton Turkle
- *Goldilocks and the Three Bears* retold by James Marshall
- *Growl! A Book About Bears* by Melvin Berger
- *We're Going on a Bear Hunt* by Michael Rosen

## The Bear Necessities

Choose from this cross-curricular selection of bear-related activities to build a terrific take-home bag.

| Skill—Activity | Title | Materials |
|---|---|---|
| Reading for information—game | "Make Tracks With Bear Facts!" | copy each of pages 16 and 17, copy of *Growl! A Book About Bears*, 2 plastic bear counters |
| Recalling information—game | "Pairs of Bears" | white construction paper copy of page 18 |
| Reading—craft | "Bear Hug Poem" "Bear Hug Hat" | tan construction paper copy each of pages 19 and 20 |
| Vocabulary—cooking | "'Bear-y' Delicious Biscuits" | copy of page 21, copy of *Blueberries for Sal* |

## Bear Bonuses

- For added interest, enclose a packet of instant oatmeal and a note that reads "Enjoy a 'bear-y' good breakfast, compliments of Goldilocks."

- Include a note asking parents to first read aloud *We're Going on a Bear Hunt* and then hide a favorite teddy bear. Encourage parents to lead the family on an adventurous bear hunt!

# Make Tracks With Bear Facts!

**Parent note:** Read aloud the enclosed nonfiction book *Growl! A Book About Bears* for some "paws-atively" factual fun! Have your child remove the accompanying sheet from the bag. Then play this game for two players (or two teams). Assist with reading the cards or finding the answers in the book as necessary.

### Directions:

1. Cut apart the cards and put them in a pile. Put the answer key nearby.

2. Put the plastic bears on Start.

3. In turn, have each player read the top card. Say if it is true or false.

4. Check the answer by the key. If correct, move forward one space. If incorrect, do nothing. Put the card on the bottom of the pile.

5. The first player to reach the bee tree wins.

START

**Parent note:** Use with the game on the accompanying sheet.

## Game Cards

| | |
|---|---|
| 1. A grizzly bear eats more than you do. | 2. A grizzly bear can be longer than a sofa. |
| 3. Polar bears only eat green plants. | 4. Eating lots of food helps a polar bear stay warm. |
| 5. Sun bears are sometimes called honey bears. | 6. Sun bears are big, big bears. |
| 7. Sloth bears are fast. | 8. Giant pandas eat bamboo. |
| 9. Giant pandas have two fingers on each front paw. | 10. A bear's nose is called a snout. |
| 11. Some bears can smell a person a mile away. | 12. Bears cannot stand on their hind legs. |
| 13. Bears never get angry. | 14. Claws always stick out on a bear's paws. |
| 15. A bear's winter home is a den. | 16. Bears never wake up in the winter. |
| 17. A baby bear is called a pup. | 18. Baby bears are often born in winter. |
| 19. Cubs sometimes stay with their mothers for many years. | 20. Mother bears teach their cubs to find food. |

### Answer Key

1. True
2. True
3. False; Polar bears eat mostly seals.
4. True
5. True
6. False; Sun bears are the smallest bears.
7. False; Sloth bears are slow.
8. True
9. False; Giant pandas have six fingers on each of their front paws.
10. True
11. True
12. False; Bears can stand on two legs.
13. False; Bears can get angry.
14. True
15. True
16. False; Bears sometimes wake up on warm winter days.
17. False; A baby bear is called a cub.
18. True
19. True
20. True

# Pairs of Bears

**Parent note:** Encourage your child to think about the different types of bears and what they look like. Then help your child read and follow the directions below to play this memory game with a partner.

## Directions:

1. Color the cards.
2. Cut apart the cards.
3. Mix them up and scatter them facedown.
4. Take turns flipping over two cards.
   If they match, keep them.
   If they don't, flip them back over.
5. When all the pairs are matched, the game is over.
   The winner is the player with more pairs.

©The Education Center, Inc. • *It's in the Bag!* • TEC4100

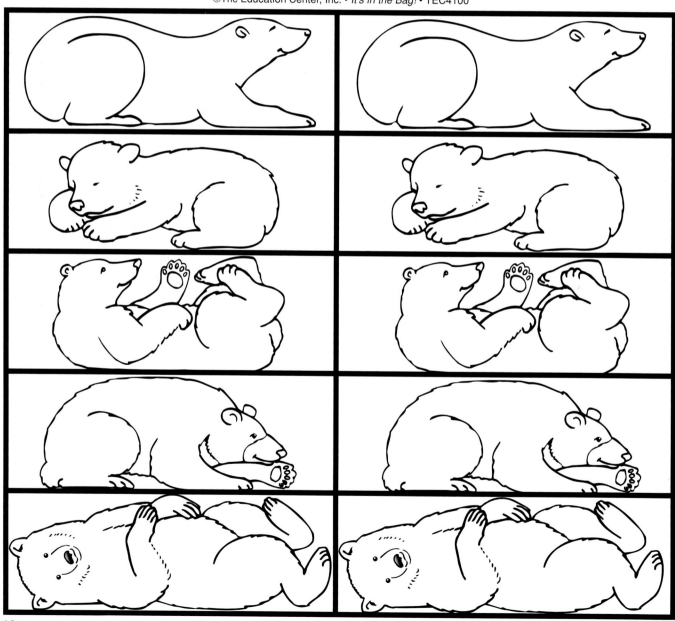

# Bear Hug Poem

There is one bear who's warm and snug.
He's always very ready
To be picked up with a great big hug.
Of course, he is my Teddy!

**Parent note:** Even though a teddy bear isn't a real bear, it's still a favorite! Read the poem with your child. Then help him or her use the arm patterns below with the accompanying sheet to make a bear hug hat.

bear arms

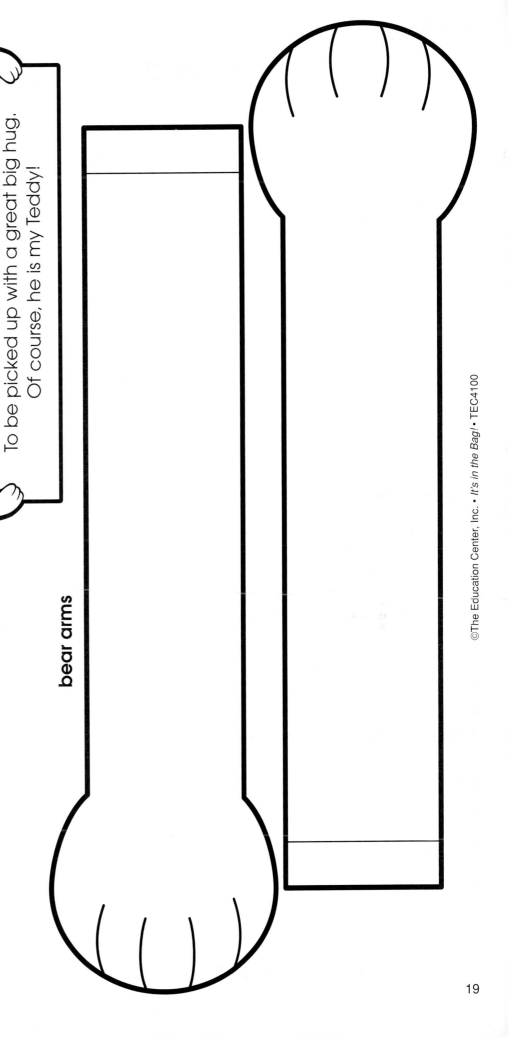

# Bear Hug Hat

**Directions:**

1. Cut out the bear's head and arms.
2. Tape the arms and the poem to the body.
3. Ask an adult to staple the arms so that the hat fits you.

Finished sample

Step 2

Tape here.

Tape here.

# "Bear-y" Delicious Biscuits

**Parent note:** Read aloud Robert McCloskey's classic, *Blueberries for Sal.* Then read and prepare the recipe below with your child, paying special attention to the bold-faced vocabulary words. For baking times and temperatures, follow the package directions. Enjoy these delicious biscuits as a family cooking experience!

**Ingredients for eight:**
can refrigerated biscuits
fresh or frozen blueberries

**Topping:**
$^1/_4$ c. melted butter or
margarine
$^1/_3$ c. honey
2 tbsp. orange juice

**Utensils and supplies:**
baking sheet
plastic knife
small bowl
spoon

## Directions to make one:

1. Cut a piece of dough as shown.
Place one piece **on** the baking sheet.

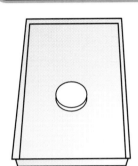

2. **Cut** the other piece in half.
Cut one of those pieces in half again.

3. Roll each of the cut pieces (except the one on the baking sheet) into a ball.

4. Use the balls to make the bear's ears and snout.

5. Finish the face with blueberries.

6. Make more **bear** biscuits the same way.

7. Bake the biscuits.

8. **Put** the topping ingredients in the bowl.
Stir until smooth.

9. Dip each biscuit into the topping.
Eat!

# A Birthday Bash

Happy birthday! Youngsters and their families will make wishes and blow out candles with this birthday-filled activity bag.

## Happy Birthday Books

Wrap up birthday reading with some of these special titles!

- *A Birthday for Frances* by Russell Hoban
- *Bunny Cakes* by Rosemary Wells
- *Carl's Birthday* by Alexandra Day
- *Happy Birthday, Dear Duck* by Eve Bunting
- *Henry and Mudge and the Best Day of All* by Cynthia Rylant

## Party Favors

Package a selection of these activities into a terrific take-home party bag.

| Skill—Activity | Title | Materials |
|---|---|---|
| Writing—booklet | "Birthday Wishes" | copy each of pages 23, 24, and 25 |
| Descriptive words—banner | "Birthday Banner" | copy of page 26, 22" length of yarn, four 12" lengths of colorful crepe paper streamer |
| Vocabulary—cooking | "Very Vanilla Ice Cream" | copy of the top of page 27, quart-size resealable freezer bag, gallon-size resealable freezer bag |
| Following directions—craft | "Happy Birthday Hat" | copy of the bottom of page 27, paper plate cut and hole-punched as shown, 9" x 12" sheet of construction paper, two 12" lengths of yarn |
| Reading for details—logic puzzle | "Which One Shall I Open First?" | copy of page 28 |

## Icing on the Cake

- Send home a note suggesting a family field trip to a neighborhood bakery to watch a baker decorate a fancy cake.
- Enclose an invitation for each family to bake and decorate a cake together. If desired, include a Betty Crocker Stir 'n Bake cake mix.

**booklet cover**

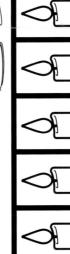

# Birthday Wishes

---

Skill: *Writing—booklet*

### Directions:

1. Color the booklet cover and candles.

2. Cut them out.

3. Glue candles on the cover to match your age.

4. Cut out the other booklet pages.

5. Write to finish the sentence starter on each page.

6. Draw a picture on each page.

7. Stack the pages in order.

8. Staple them to make a booklet.

**candles**

# Booklet Pages 1 and 2

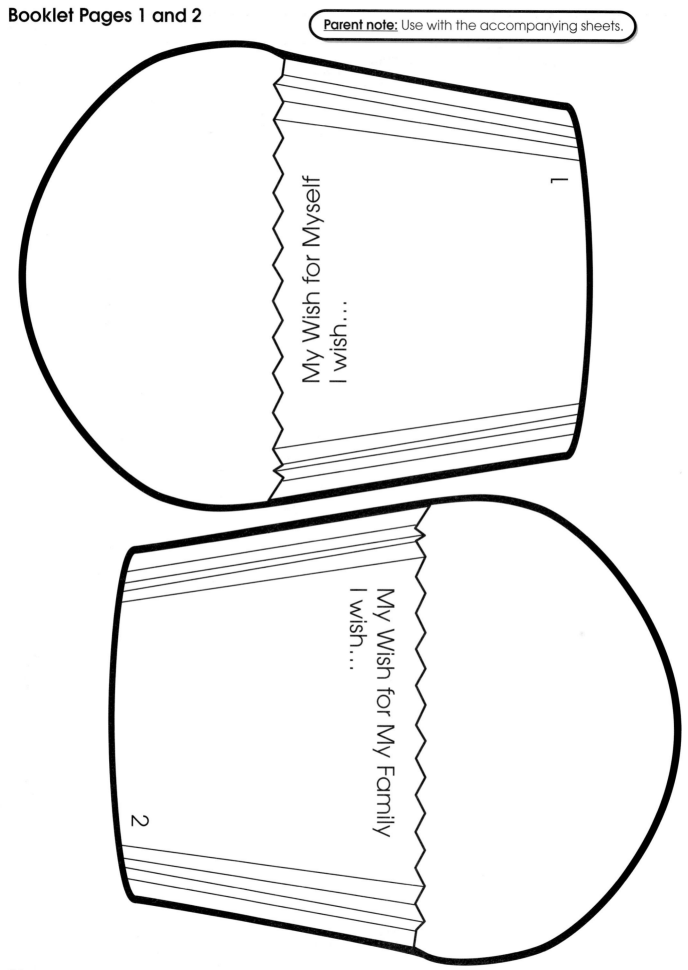

My Wish for Myself
I wish....

1

My Wish for My Family
I wish....

2

# Booklet Pages 3 and 4

**Parent note:** Use with the accompanying sheets.

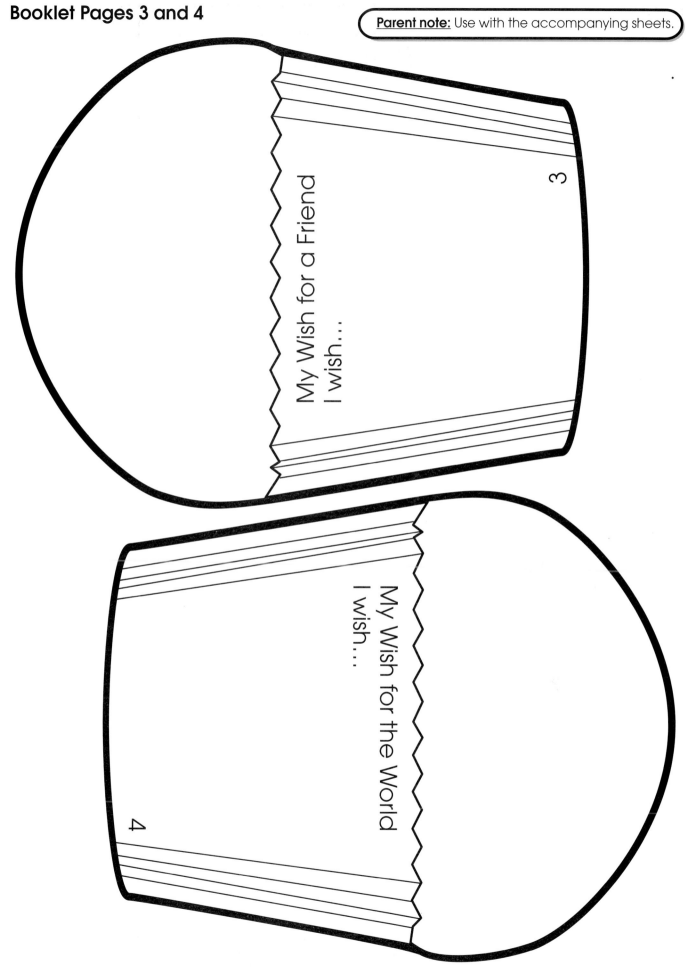

My Wish for a Friend
I wish....

3

My Wish for the World
I wish....

4

**Skill:** *Descriptive words—banner*

# Birthday Banner

**Parent note:** Talk with your child about his or her special qualities. Help your youngster list words that describe himself or herself. Then have your child gather the yarn and streamers from the bag. Provide necessary assistance as your child reads the directions below and completes this festive birthday banner.

## Directions:

1. Cut out the banner.
2. Write your age and name.
3. Write one word from your list on each gift.
4. Color the banner.
5. Glue the yarn to make a hanger.
6. Glue streamers to the back of the banner.

**Making the hanger:**

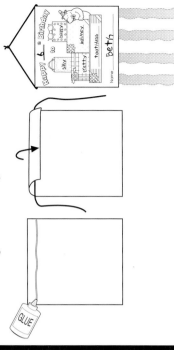

GLUE

Fold here.

# Happy
# —th Birthday
to

Name _____

©The Education Center, Inc. • *It's in the Bag!* • TEC4100

# Very Vanilla Ice Cream

**Parent note:** Ask your child if anything tastes as good as homemade ice cream. Then have your child remove the resealable bags from the bag. Help your child read and follow the directions below, paying special attention to the boldfaced vocabulary words. Make and eat this frosty ice-cream treat as a family cooking experience.

**Ingredients:**
1/2 c. whole **milk**
1 tbsp. **sugar**
1/4 tsp. vanilla

**Utensils and supplies:**
gallon-size resealable freezer bag
quart-size resealable freezer bag
2 c. **ice** cubes
1/2 c. table salt
spoon

## Directions:

1. Pour the ice-cream ingredients in the small bag.
2. **Seal** the bag.
3. Put the ice and salt in the large bag.
4. Place the small bag inside the large one.
5. Seal the large bag.
6. **Shake** the bags for about five minutes.
7. Use a spoon to **eat** this yummy ice cream straight from the bag!

©The Education Center, Inc. • *It's in the Bag!* • TEC4100

---

# Happy Birthday Hat

**Parent note:** It just wouldn't be a party without funny hats! Have your child gather the precut paper plate, construction paper, and yarn from the bag. Fold the plate's center section up as shown. Then assist your child in reading the directions below and completing the steps to make his or her personalized birthday hat.

## Directions:

1. Trace your hands.
2. Cut out the hand shapes.
3. Show how old you are with your fingers.
4. Glue the hands to show your age.
5. Glue the hands to the plate.
6. Write "Happy Birthday" and your name on the plate.
7. Tie yarn to each side to make a hat.
8. Dance around wearing your birthday hat!

©The Education Center, Inc. • *It's in the Bag!* • TEC4100

# Which One Shall I Open First?

| First | Second | Third | Fourth | Fifth |

## Clues:

The third gift is striped.

The gift with flowers on it is in the space to the left of the striped gift.

The fifth gift does not have corners.

The checkered gift is between the striped gift and the dotted gift.

The gift with balloons on it is next to the flowered gift bag.

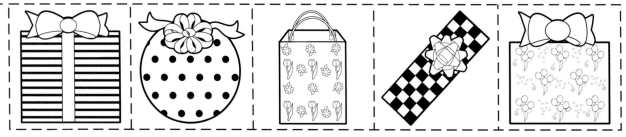

# Bug Mania!

From grasshoppers to flies to ladybugs and more—your young-sters and their families will go buggy over these literacy activities!

## Catch These Bug Books!

Tuck several of these books in the bag to get families all aflutter over books!
- *Bugs! Bugs! Bugs!* by Bob Barner
- *From Caterpillar to Butterfly* by Deborah Heiligman
- *The Grouchy Ladybug* by Eric Carle
- *Honeybee's Busy Day* by Richard Fowler
- *I Know an Old Lady Who Swallowed a Fly* by Nadine Bernard Westcott

## Much Ado About Insects

Give your students and their families insight into insects with this collection of critter activities.

| Skill—Activity | Title | Materials |
|---|---|---|
| Beginning consonants—writing | "Buggy Over Words" | copy of page 30 |
| Ending consonants—game | "Catching Critters" | copy of page 31, set of 20 index cards (each programmed with a different consonant) |
| Retelling a story—story bag | "Oh My—It's a Fly!" | white construction paper copy each of pages 32 and 33, copy of the book *I Know an Old Lady Who Swallowed a Fly*, lunch-size paper bag |
| Vocabulary—labeling | "Invent an Insect" | copy of page 34, sheet of light-colored construction paper, variety of craft supplies |

## More to Buzz About

- For added interest, enclose a note en-couraging parents to take their child on a bug hunt (with a magnifying glass and a small plastic jar with a hole-punched lid). Encourage the family to identify the parts of each bug after it has been safely captured. Make sure to include a gentle reminder to release the critters immediately after observation.

- Tuck a spiral-bound notebook into the bag with a note encouraging each family to write a poem about bugs. Invite each family to read and enjoy the other poems in the notebook. Keep the notebook in the bag to create a family-written poetry book.

29

# Buggy Over Words

## Directions:

1. Point to a bug.
   Read its name.
2. Say its beginning sound.
   Write its beginning letter on the blank.
3. Write three new words with the same beginning sound and letter.
4. Repeat for the other two bugs.

**bee** _____

1. _____
2. _____
3. _____

**moth** _____

1. _____
2. _____
3. _____

**ladybug** _____

1. _____
2. _____
3. _____

# Catching Critters

**Parent note:** Here's a fun two-player game that will help reinforce your child's understanding of ending sounds and letters. Each player will need a different-colored crayon. Have your child remove the letter cards from the bag and place them facedown on a table. Help your child read and follow the directions below to play the game. During play, help your child reshuffle the cards if necessary.

## Directions:

1. In turn, pick a letter card.
   Say the sound.
2. Look at the bugs below.
   Find a bug that has a picture with the same ending sound.
   Color it.
   If there is no bug for that letter, your turn is over.
   If the bug is already colored, your turn is over.
3. The game is over when all the bugs are colored.
   The player with the most colored bugs wins.

# Oh My—It's a Fly!

**Parent note:** Read aloud the enclosed story *I Know an Old Lady Who Swallowed a Fly*. Then help your child read and follow the directions to complete the story bag. (In Step 4, be sure to assist your child in cutting out the mouth.) To extend this activity, have your child draw, color, and then cut out a variety of insects (ladybugs, crickets, etc.). Then have him or her use the cut-outs to tell a new version of the story.

## Directions:

1. Color the face and cut it out.
2. Open the paper bag.
3. Glue the face to the front of the bag.
4. Cut on the dotted line to make a mouth.
5. Color the animals and cut them out.
6. Tell the story.

©The Education Center, Inc. • *It's in the Bag!* • TEC4100

**Parent note:** Use with the accompanying sheet.

fly

spider

bird

cat

dog

goat

cow

horse

# Invent an Insect

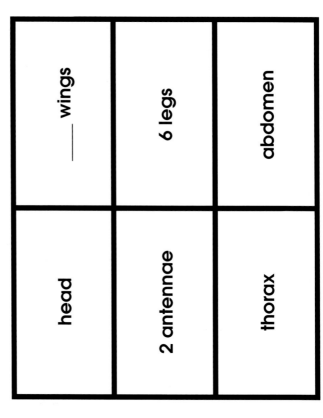

**Parent note:** After reading a nonfiction book about insects, talk to your child about insects and their body parts. Then have your child remove the construction paper and craft supplies from the bag. Help your child read and follow the directions to create an imaginary insect.

## Directions:

1. Look at the ant.
2. Name its body parts.
3. Think of a pretend insect.
4. Look at the construction paper.
   Draw three **body parts.**
   Draw six **legs.**
   Draw two **antennae** on its head if you like.
   Draw **wings** if you like.
5. Color and decorate your insect.
6. Look at the words below.
   Cut them out.
7. Glue each word next to its matching body part on your insect.
8. Write your insect's name.

| head | _____ wings |
|---|---|
| 2 antennae | 6 legs |
| thorax | abdomen |

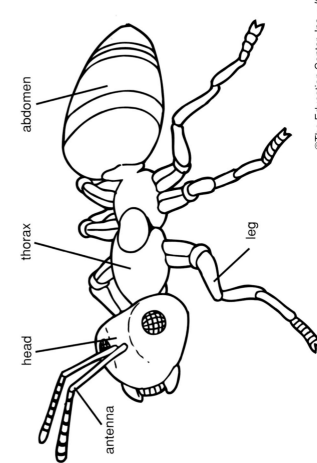

# The Circus Comes to Town!

Here for a few nights only, this circus-themed bag will help put literacy in the center ring!

## Featured Performers
Shine the spotlight on this collection of circus-related literature by including some of these books in the bag.

- *Circus* by Lois Ehlert
- *The Circus Alphabet* by Linda Bronson
- *Harold's Circus* by Crockett Johnson
- *If I Ran the Circus* by Dr. Suess
- *Olivia Saves the Circus* by Ian Falconer

## Under the Big Top
Don the ringmaster's hat and choose from the following circus-themed activities for this big top bag.

| Skill—Activity | Title | Materials |
| --- | --- | --- |
| Writing—craft | "Funny Face" | copy each of pages 36 and 37 |
| Drawing conclusions—logic puzzle | "Clowning Around" | copy of page 38 |
| Oral language—song | "The Circus" | copy of page 39 |
| Critical thinking—game | "In the Spotlight" | copy of page 40, 2' length of yarn, 8 paper clips in 2 different colors |

## Encore, Encore!
- Enrich the circus experience by including a package of microwave popcorn and a circus movie, such as *Kids Love the Circus,* in the bag.

- For more fun, enclose a spiral-bound notebook with a note encouraging families to create a family circus performance that highlights individual talents. Invite each family to share its performance with the class by writing and illustrating a description of its circus.

# Funny Face

**Parent note:** Clowns can look happy, sad, or anywhere in between. Ask your child what type of clown he or she prefers. Have your child remove the accompanying page from the bag. Then help your child read and follow the directions to create a one-of-a-kind clown.

## Directions:

1. Your clown needs two eyes.
   He needs a nose.
   He needs a mouth too.
2. Pick out the ones you like.
3. Color and cut them out.
4. Glue them to the face.
5. Look below the clown.
   Read.
   Write to complete the sentence.

No clowning around—I'm the best in town!
My face looks…

**Parent note:** Use with the accompanying sheet.

eyes

noses

mouths

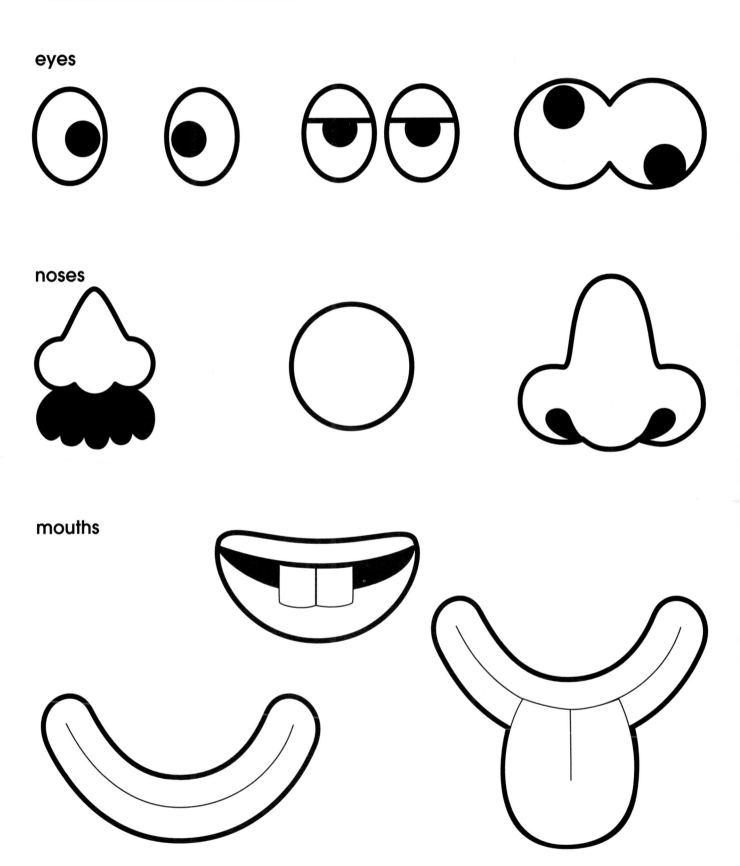

# Clowning Around

**Parent note:** Who wants what? Help your child read and follow the directions and clues below to match each clown and object.

**Directions:**

1. Read the color words below.
2. Color each clown to match.
3. Read a clue.
   Point to the clown who is in the clue.
   Point to the thing he wants.
   Draw a line to match.
4. Repeat until each clown is correctly matched with something.

**Clues:**

Find the **blue** clown. He wants something for his head.
Find the **green** clown. He wants a pet.
Find the **red** clown. He wants a treat to eat.
Find the **yellow** clown. He wants something round.
Find the **orange** clown. He wants something new for his feet.

# The Circus

*(sung to the tune of "London Bridge")*

Chorus:
The circus has come to town,
Come to town, come to town.
The circus has come to town.
Who will we see?

Acrobats swing way up high,
Way up high, way up high.
Acrobats swing way up high.
That's who we see!
(chorus)

Funny clowns do lots of tricks,
Lots of tricks, lots of tricks.
Funny clowns do lots of tricks.
That's who we see!
(chorus)

Shaggy lions growl and roar,
Growl and roar, growl and roar.
Shaggy lions growl and roar.
That's who we see!

#  In the Spotlight

**Parent note:** Read or talk about people and things that you may see at the circus. Then remove the yarn from the bag and tie it between two objects (such as chairs) to make a tightrope. Give your child four paper clips of one color (to represent acrobats) and keep four of another color for yourself. Cut out the two cards below. Give the child's card to your child and keep the other one. Help your child read the directions, clues, and answers below.

## Directions:

1. Look at your card.
   Read sentence 1 to your partner.
   Do not read the answer.
2. Listen for the answer.
   Check your card for the correct answer.
3. If the answer is correct, your partner puts an acrobat on the tightrope.
   If the answer is incorrect, your partner does nothing.
4. Listen as a clue is read to you.
   Answer the question.
5. If the answer is correct, put an acrobat on the tightrope.
   If your answer is incorrect, do nothing.
6. Keep taking turns reading and answering.
7. The game ends when all the acrobats are on the tightrope.

©The Education Center, Inc. • *It's in the Bag!* • TEC4100

---

## Who or What Am I?
(child's card)
1. I'm pink and sweet to eat. What am I? *(cotton candy)*
2. I keep a trunk with me. What am I? *(an elephant)*
3. I swing way up high. Who am I? *(an acrobat)*
4. I call out each act. Who am I? *(the ringmaster)*
5. I do silly tricks. Who am I? *(a clown)*
6. I have fur, but I'm not Teddy. What am I? *(a bear)*

---

## Who or What Am I?
(partner's card)
1. I gallop around the ring. Some people like to stand on my back. What am I?
   *(a horse)*
2. Hold on tight! I am colorful and filled with air. What am I? *(a balloon)*
3. Give me a banana or two, and I'll perform a trick for you! What am I?
   *(a monkey)*
4. I look like a giant tent. People come inside to see shows. What am I?
   *(the big top)*
5. Watch your balance! I am thin and hard to walk on. What am I? *(a tightrope)*
6. I have large pointy teeth and a ferocious roar! What am I? *(a lion)*

©The Education Center, Inc. • *It's in the Bag!* • TEC4100

# Splashes of Color

Brighten youngsters' learning experiences with this colorful collection of literacy-rich activities.

## Red, Yellow, Green, Blue...

...These vibrant books are just waiting for you!

- *Brown Bear, Brown Bear, What Do You See?* by Bill Martin Jr.
- *Elmer's Colors* by David McKee
- *Little Blue and Little Yellow* by Leo Lionni
- *Mary Wore Her Red Dress and Henry Wore His Green Sneakers* adapted by Merle Peek
- *Seven Blind Mice* by Ed Young

## Colorful Connections

Stir up some color-filled learning by choosing from this array of ideas.

| Skill—Activity | Title | Materials |
| --- | --- | --- |
| Color words—poem | "Colors in Motion" | copy of page 42 |
| Color words—booklet | "Colors All Around" | copy of page 43, 5 sheets of 5 1/2" x 8" white paper, old magazine |
| Color words, critical thinking—game | "Color Concentration" | construction paper copy of page 44 |
| Color words—game | "Rainbow Row" | white construction paper copy of page 45, two 2-ounce bags of original Skittles candy |
| Following directions—color experiment | "Cool New Colors" | white construction paper copy of page 46; small plastic plate; paintbrush; yellow, red, and blue watercolor paints |

## More Splashes of Color

- Send home a note encouraging each parent and child to go on a color hunt. Tell the parent to have his child pick a specific color. Then have them take a walk together around their neighborhood and point out all the color-specific items that they see.

- Tuck a blank graph into the bag and have each parent help her child graph the colors in the child's bedroom. For example, how many blue things are there? Green things? Invite the child to share his completed graph.

41

# Colors in Motion

Colors in motion, oh, so bright.
Colors in motion, such a sight!

Wiggle your nose if you're wearing blue.
Clap your hands. Touch your shoe.

Jump up and down if you're wearing white.
Skip to the left. Skip to the right.

Take three steps if you're wearing pink.
Shout, "Hooray!" Now give a wink.

Blink your eyes if you're wearing green.
Act like a clown, then a jumping bean.

Turn around if you're wearing red.
Shrug your shoulders. Nod your head.

Bend your knee if you're wearing brown.
Shake your arms; then sit right down.

Colors in motion, touch the floor.
Let's do it again, just once more!

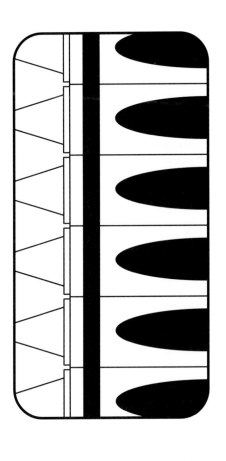

# COLORS ALL AROUND

by

_____

©The Education Center, Inc.

---

**Skill:** _Color words—booklet_

# Colors All Around

**Parent note:** This colorful booklet is just right to strengthen your child's color-recognition skills. Have your child remove the white paper and magazine from the bag. Help your child color and cut out the cover at the right and then stack the white paper pages behind the cover and staple them. Then guide your child in reading and following the directions below to complete the booklet.

**Directions:**

**Page 1:** Write the word _yellow._
Cut out a picture of something yellow.
Glue it to the page.

**Page 2:** Write the word _green._
Cut out a picture of something green.
Glue it to the page.

**Page 3:** Write the word _blue._
Cut out a picture of something blue.
Glue it to the page.

**Page 4:** Write the word _red._
Cut out a picture of something red.
Glue it to the page.

**Page 5:** Write the word _orange._
Cut out a picture of something orange.
Glue it to the page.

**Finished Sample**

43

# Color Concentration

| | | | |
|---|---|---|---|
| I am red. | I am blue. | strawberry — red | log — brown |
| I am orange. | I am brown. | chick — yellow | frog — green |
| I am yellow. | I am green. | leaf — blue | grapes — purple |
| We are purple. | I am black and white. | skunk — black and white | orange — orange |

**Parent note:** Talk with your child about the different colors he or she sees in nature, such as green grass and a blue sky. Then help your child read and follow the directions below to prepare and play the game. Enjoy playing a round or two of Color Concentration (played like a traditional memory game)!

**Directions:**

1. Look at the pictures on the cards. Color them.

2. Cut out all the cards.

3. Turn the cards facedown. Mix them up. Spread them out.

4. Turn over two cards. If they match, keep them. If they do not match, turn them back over.

5. Try to find the most matching pairs!

# Rainbow Row

**Parent note:** Here's a sweet variation of bingo to help improve your child's color-recognition skills. Have your child remove the bags of Skittles candy from the bag, then give one to his or her partner. Help your child read and follow the directions below to prepare and play the game.

## Directions:

1. Cut out the gameboards. Give one to your partner.
2. Open your bag of Skittles candy.
3. On your turn, reach into the bag without looking. Take one candy. Look at your card. If the candy matches one of the color words, put it on your card.
4. When you have five in a row, say, "Rainbow!"
5. Eat the candy!

**Gameboard 1**

| red    | purple | green  | red    | red    |
|--------|--------|--------|--------|--------|
| yellow | orange | purple | green  | orange |
| yellow | green  | red    | purple | yellow |
| orange | red    | yellow | red    | green  |
| green  | purple | orange | green  | green  |

©The Education Center, Inc.

**Gameboard 2**

| red    | purple | green  | red    | red    |
|--------|--------|--------|--------|--------|
| yellow | orange | purple | green  | orange |
| yellow | green  | red    | purple | green  |
| orange | red    | yellow | red    | yellow |
| green  | purple | orange | purple | green  |

©The Education Center, Inc.

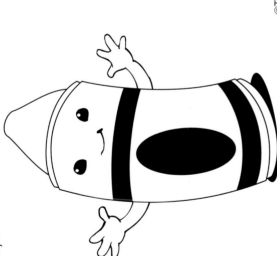

# Cool New Colors

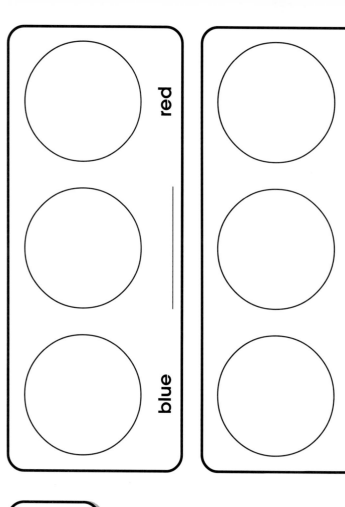

blue      _____      red

blue      _____      yellow

red      _____      yellow

**Parent note:** It's true—yellow and blue *do* make green! Before beginning this paint-mixing activity, cover a workspace with newspaper or paper towels. Have your child get a small cup of water and then remove the plate, paint, and paintbrush from the bag. Help your child read and follow the directions below to make new colors.

## Directions:

1. Look at the color words below.
   Read them.
   These are *primary* colors.

2. Look at the first box.
   Read the color words.

3. Put those two paint colors on the plate.
   Paint those two circles in the box.

4. What will happen if you mix those colors?
   Try it. Mix these two colors on the plate.
   Paint the middle circle with the new color.
   Write its name.

5. Repeat Steps 2, 3, and 4 with the other boxes.
   Cool! You have made *secondary* colors.

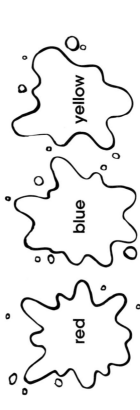

red      blue      yellow

# Calling All Kinfolk!

Calling moms, dads, siblings, and grandparents too! This family-themed bag will be a hit with your crew!

## Family Connections

These books are just right for some cuddly reading with one family member or the whole clan.

- *Arthur's Baby* by Marc Brown
- *Bigmama's* by Donald Crews
- *Julius: The Baby of the World* by Kevin Henkes
- *Mama Elizabeti* by Stephanie Stuve-Bodeen
- *The Relatives Came* by Cynthia Rylant
- *Tell Me Again About the Night I Was Born* by Jamie Lee Curtis

## "Fun-tastic" Family Activities

Pack a bag full of these fabulous family activities!

| Skill—Activity | Title | Materials |
|---|---|---|
| Action words—booklet | "My Family Makes Me Happy!" | white construction paper copy of page 48, copy of page 49, 2 sheets of blank paper |
| Classification—chart | "Picture This!" | copy of page 50, 12" x 18" sheet of light-colored construction paper |
| Classification—menu | "It's Dinnertime!" | copy of page 51, large paper plate, several old magazines |
| Descriptive words—poem | "What's It All About?" | copy of page 52 |
| Observation, values—incentive | "Pass It On" | copy of page 53, 2 sheets of yellow construction paper |

## Family Ties

- For added interest, enclose a copy of the familiar song "The Wheels on the Bus" with a note inviting the family to sing it together. Encourage them to use the rhythm and tune to create a unique verse for each family member, such as "The grandpa on the bus goes snore, snore, snore."
- Include a note inviting the family to have a Portrait Gallery Night, when family members draw pictures of each other and then display them in a high-traffic area of the home.
- Promote oral language skills by enclosing a list of family interview questions, such as "What is your favorite family activity?" and "What's your favorite room in the house?" Invite family members to interview one another.

# My Family Makes Me Happy!

**Parent note:** Talk with your child about fun activities you enjoy as a family. Then have your child remove the accompanying sheet and blank paper from the bag. Assist your child in coloring and cutting out the booklet cover. Next, help your child trace the cover onto each sheet of blank paper and then cut out the tracings. Show your child how to stack the pages behind the cover and fold them on the dotted line. Staple the pages to make a booklet; then help your child read and follow the directions below to complete the writing activity.

### Directions:

1. Cut out the banners below.
2. Open the booklet.
   Look at the first page.
3. Glue on a banner.
4. Read the words.
   Think about one thing your family enjoys doing together.
   Write to fill in the blank.
   Draw a picture to go with your sentence.
5. Turn the page.
6. Repeat Steps 3–5 until all the banners have been used.
7. Read your booklet to your family.

| We _____ together. | We _____ together. |
| We _____ together. | We _____ together. |

We _____ together.

**Booklet Cover**

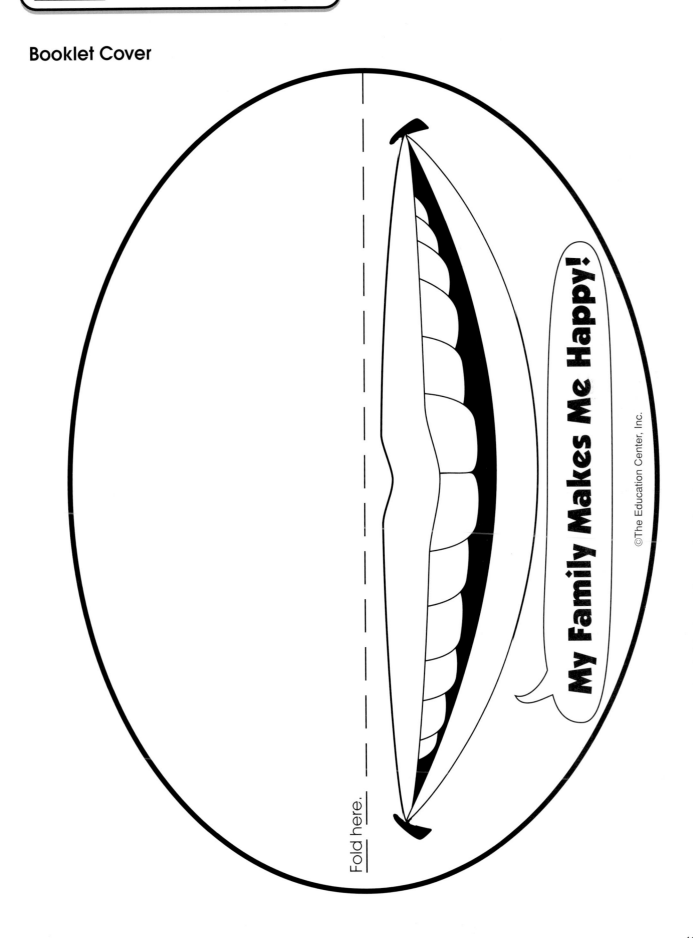

Fold here.

My Family Makes Me Happy!

©The Education Center, Inc.

# Picture This!

**Parent note:** Families come in all shapes and sizes, and all can be wonderful! Talk with your child about different types of family members, such as brothers, aunts, grandfathers, and so forth. Have your child remove the construction paper from the bag. Then help your child read and follow the directions below to complete the activity. **Tips:** In Step 4 you may wish to assist your child in using objects to group and count family members accurately. If you need more space, add another sheet of paper to the chart. Display the finished project where it can be enjoyed by all.

## Directions:

1. Write one type of family member in the first chart block.
   Write how many of that type of family member.
2. Write one type of family member in the second chart block.
   Write how many of that type of family member.
3. Repeat until all the chart blocks are full.
4. Add all of the numbers.
5. Write the total.
   Read the sentence.
6. Cut out the chart.
7. Glue it onto construction paper.
8. Draw and label your family.

| Family Members | How Many? | Family Members | How Many? |
|---|---|---|---|
|  |  |  |  |
|  |  |  |  |
|  |  |  |  |
|  |  |  |  |
|  |  |  |  |

There are _____ people in my family.

# It's Dinnertime!

**Parent note:** Since dinnertime is often important family time, get your child in on the planning. Discuss with your child the kinds of healthy foods you use to prepare a family meal. Then have your child remove the magazines and paper plate from the bag. Help your child read and follow the directions below to create a dinner menu. For added fun, invite your child to help you prepare a meal similar to the one in the completed activity.

## Directions:

1. Read the types of foods on the menu below.
2. Look at the magazines.
   Find and cut out a food picture for each food type.
   Glue the pictures to the plate.
3. Write each food you have found on the menu.
4. Cut out the menu.
   Glue it to the back of the plate.

# Tonight's Dinner Menu

Main dish: _____

Bread: _____

Vegetable: _____

Vegetable or fruit: _____

Drink: _____

Dessert: _____

# What's It All About?

**Parent note:** It's all about family! Brainstorm with your child a list of words and phrases that describe your family. Then help your child read and follow the directions below to write a simple poem.

## Directions:

1. Look at the first line.
   Think of a word or phrase that begins with the letter *F* and describes your family.
   Write it.

2. Look at the second line.
   Think of a word or phrase that begins with the letter *A* and describes your family.
   Write it.

3. Continue until all the lines are finished.

4. Read your poem to your family.

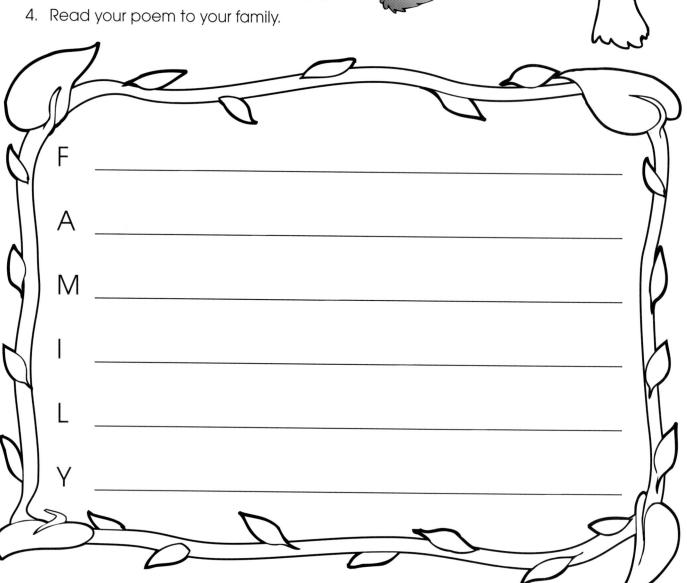

F _____

A _____

M _____

I _____

L _____

Y _____

# Pass It On

**Parent note:** Talk with your child about your family's values; then enjoy a star-studded activity that will have family members noticing the good in one another. Direct your child to remove the yellow paper from the bag. Next, assist him or her in preparing a batch of stars by cutting out the pattern below, then tracing it a desired number of times onto the yellow paper. Have your child cut out the stars, neatly copy the words, and then gather the family together. As a group, discuss your family's values. Invite your child to write one value on each star and display them in your home. Then help him or her read and follow the directions below to complete the stars.

## Directions:

1. Watch your family.
   When a person shows a family value, get that star.
2. Write that person's name and the day on the star.
3. Put the star back in the display so everyone can see it.
4. Ask that person to repeat Steps 1–4.

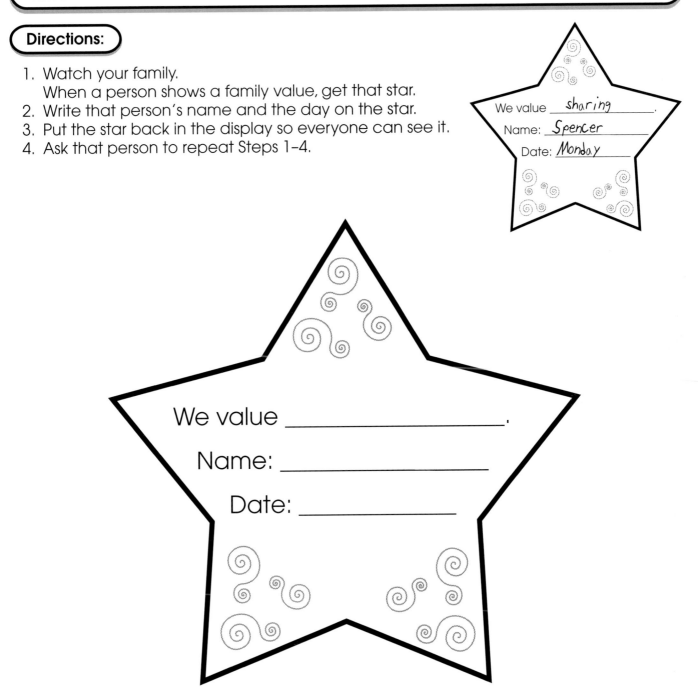

We value ___sharing___.
Name: _Spencer_
Date: _Monday_

We value _____.
Name: _____
Date: _____

# Flower Power

Youngsters will bloom with enthusiasm when they take home this bouquet of flower activities!

### Dig In!

Cultivate family reading by planting a variety of these bright books in the bag.

- *Alison's Zinnia* by Anita Lobel
- *Flower Garden* by Eve Bunting
- *Sunflower House* by Eve Bunting

## Garden Essentials

Pick and choose from these activities to create a beautiful bouquet for each family!

| Skill—Activity | Title | Materials |
|---|---|---|
| Vocabulary—patterns | "Flower Path Patterns" | copy of page 55 |
| Reading for pleasure—incentive | "Budding Readers" | copy of page 56 |
| Reading for details—sequencing | "Grow, Flower, Grow!" | copy of page 57, blank sheet of copy paper |
| Vocabulary—game | "Flower Lotto" | white construction paper copy each of pages 58 and 59, paper bag containing 18 sunflower seeds |

### Special Sprouts

- Enclose a large sheet of drawing paper with a note inviting each family to design and draw its own flower garden.

- Provide a list of interesting public flower gardens, arboretums, and parks in your area. Encourage families to visit these places and enjoy the flowers.

# Flower Path Patterns

**Parent note:** If you have a copy of Anita Lobel's *Alison's Zinnia*, reread it with your child to introduce this activity. While reading, encourage your child to notice the different kinds of flowers in the story. Next, have him or her gather five different flower-colored crayons. Invite your child to look at the grid below and then use the crayons to color each type of flower a different color. Help your child read and follow the directions below to complete the flower patterns.

## Directions:

1. Cut out the cards.
   Read each flower name.
2. Read the first flower pattern.
3. Find a flower to complete it.
   Glue that card in the correct spot.
4. Continue reading and completing each pattern.

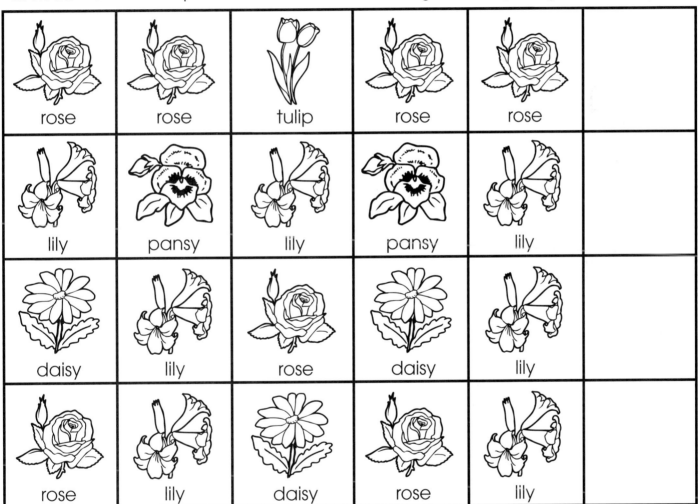

# Budding Readers

Help me plant a flower seed,
One that grows as I read and read.
Add a petal each time we look
At a different storybook!

**Parent note:** This activity provides a fun way to keep track of the books your child reads. Help your child read and follow the directions below to complete the reading flower. If desired, have your child add a paper stem and leaves. Display the finished flower in your home.

## Directions:

1. Read the poem at the right.
   Cut it out.
2. Read a favorite book with someone.
3. Write the book's title on a petal.
   Cut it out.
4. Glue the petal to the back of the poem.
5. Repeat Steps 2–4 until the flower has five petals.
6. If you wish, color your flower.

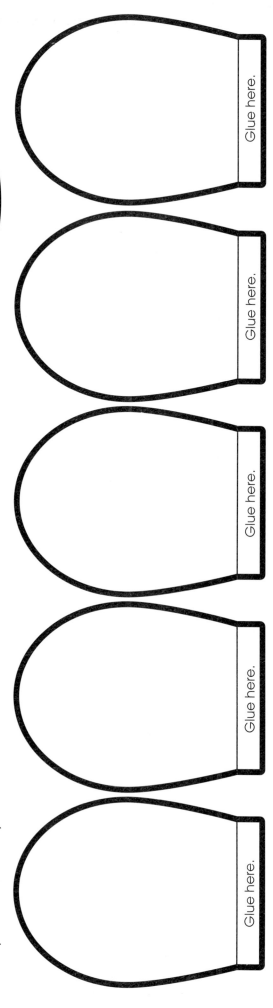

# Grow, Flower, Grow!

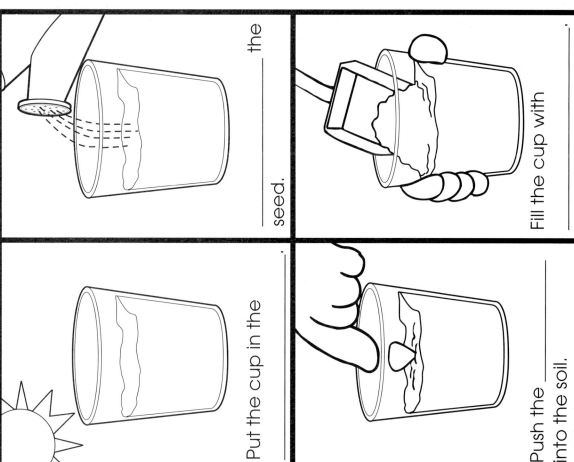

the _____ seed.

Fill the cup with _____.

Put the cup in the _____.

Push the _____ into the soil.

**Parent note:** Just how do flowers grow? Have your child remove the blank paper from the bag. Help him or her read and follow the directions below to complete the growth sequence. If you have some flower seeds at home, invite your child to plant them and watch them grow.

## Directions:

1. Read a sentence.
   Think about the missing word.
2. Write it in the blank.
   Use the word bank to help.
3. Repeat Steps 1 and 2 until all the sentences are complete.
4. Cut out the pictures.
5. Put them in order on the blank paper.
   Glue them.

PANSY

**Word Bank**

soil
sun
water
seed

# Flower Lotto

| | | | |
|---|---|---|---|
| daisy | lily | tulip | rose |
| zinnia | pansy | violet | daffodil |
| daisy | lily | tulip | rose |
| zinnia | pansy | violet | daffodil |

**Parent note:** Reread a favorite book about flowers and talk about the different names with your child. Together, look at the cards at the right and say the flower names. Have your child and his or her partner decide how to color each type of flower. Next, have your child remove the accompanying sheet from the bag. Invite your child to cut out the gameboards and the cards and then give one board to his or her partner. Guide your child and the game partner in coloring each flower on his or her board to match the cards. Ask your child to remove the paper bag and seeds from the bag; then help your child read and follow the directions below to play the game. If more cards are needed, simply help your child put them back in the bag, shake it, and continue play.

**Directions:**

1. Put the cards in the paper bag.
   Give each player a board.
   Count nine seeds for each player.
2. Reach into the bag and pick a card.
3. Read the card.
   Show the picture.
4. If a player has a match, he or she puts a seed on top of it.
   If there is not a match, the player does nothing.
5. The first player to cover three boxes in a row wins.
6. Put the cards back in the bag.
   Play again!

# Flower Lotto Gameboards

**Parent note:** Use with the accompanying page.

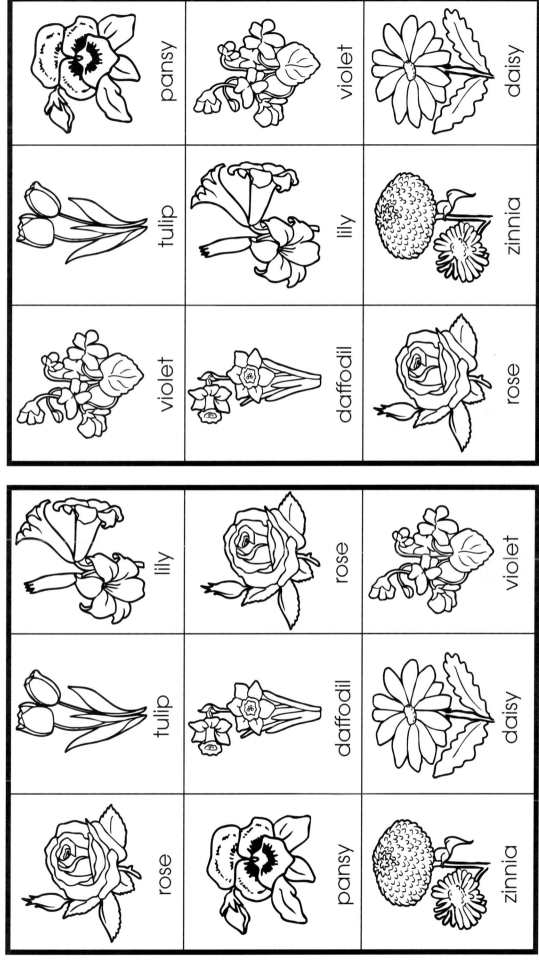

# Fabulous Friends

Pals, chums, amigos, and mates will enjoy hanging out with this cross-curricular bag of companionable activities.

## Book Buddies

Take a warmhearted look at friendship and reading skills with this selection of friendly literature.
- *Best Friends for Frances* by Russell Hoban
- *Chester's Way* by Kevin Henkes
- *Friends* by Helme Heine
- *Frog and Toad Are Friends* by Arnold Lobel
- *Poppy & Ella: 3 Stories About 2 Friends* by Jef Kaminsky

## The Gang's All Here!

Families can be friends too, so choose from the activities below to help strengthen the family-friendly bonds.

| Skill—Activity | Title | Materials |
|---|---|---|
| Storytelling—puppetry | "Friendly Puppet" | copy of the book *Frog and Toad Are Friends,* 2 white construction paper copies of page 61, paint stirrer |
| Descriptive words and phrases—craft | "We Belong Together" | copy of pages 62 and 63, two 24" lengths of yarn, 2 interlocking puzzle pieces that have been hole-punched and spray-painted white. |
| Vocabulary—game | "Crazy Checkers" | copy of page 64, resealable plastic bag containing 22 green Froot Loops cereal pieces, resealable plastic bag containing 22 red Froot Loops cereal pieces |
| Creative writing—story | "A Wonderfully Wacky Story" | copy of pages 65 and 66 |

## Best Friend Bonuses

- Enclose a note asking parents to help their child remember beloved friends by sending each of them a letter.
- Include a note inviting families to make a friendship fruit salad. Have each friend (family member) cut a portion of his favorite fruit into bite-size pieces. Mix the fruit pieces and then serve a generous helping to each friend.

# Friendly Puppet

**Parent note:** Read and discuss the book *Frog and Toad Are Friends*. Have your child remove the paint stirrer and accompanying sheet from the bag. Then help your child read and follow the directions to make a Frog and a Toad puppet. Encourage him or her to use the puppet to retell Frog and Toad's stories or to create new ones.

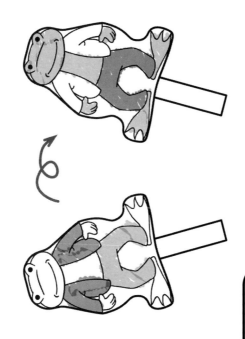

**Directions:**

1. Color one pattern to look like Frog. Cut it out.

2. Color the other pattern to look like Toad. Cut it out.

3. Glue Frog to one side of the paint stirrer. Glue Toad to the other side of the stirrer.

4. Retell the story.

# We Belong Together

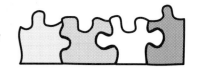

**Parent note:** Discuss with your child what makes a friend special. Next, have him or her remove from the bag the accompanying sheet, puzzle pieces, and yarn. Help your child read and follow the directions below to complete the card and puzzle-piece necklaces.

### Card directions:

1. Cut on the dotted line.

2. Fold on the long bold line.

3. Fold on the short bold line.

4. Color the cover.

5. Open the card.
   Write a friend's name inside.

6. Use each letter in the word *friend* to write about your friend.

7. Write your name and draw your picture on the back of the card.

Billy

F unny
R eally smart
I ce hockey fan
E ats ice cream
N ice to animals
D oesn't like broccoli!

### Necklace directions:

1. Color the puzzle pieces.

2. Use the yarn to make two necklaces.
   One is for you.
   One is for your friend.

3. Give the card and a necklace to your friend.
   Show your friend that you have a necklace to match.

F R I E N D

_____
(friend's name)

Made for You
By

_____
(your name)

## We Belong Together

# Crazy Checkers

**Parent note:** Friends are great for playing games! Have your child remove the bags of cereal from the bag and give one to a friend. Next, assist the pair in setting up the checkerboard below with 11 pieces of cereal each. Explain to them how to play this variation of checkers. Players take turns moving diagonally (forward) across the board on the light squares. If there is a word on a square, a player reads it before moving to that space. During a turn, a player jumps and eats his or her friend's pieces when possible. Point out the king line (the last row), and tell players that when they move a piece to that line, they can eat any one piece of their friend's cereal. The game ends when one player has eaten all his or her partner's pieces, or when one player has as many pieces as possible in the opposite king line.

| kind | | fun | | happy | | nice |
|---|---|---|---|---|---|---|
| | playful | | girl | | boy | |
| laugh | | best | | friend | | good |
| | | | | | | |
| boy | | happy | | laugh | | girl |
| | best | | nice | | friend | |
| play | | kind | | fun | | good |

 # A Wonderfully Wacky Story

**Parent note:** You never know who will make a great friend! Help your child read and follow the directions below to write and illustrate a wacky story about unlikely friends on the accompanying sheet. Encourage your youngster to use his or her imagination to develop the story aloud before writing it down. Help your child use correct ending punctuation.

**Directions:**

1. Choose one phrase from boxes one, two, and three.
2. Add other words and an ending to make a story.
3. Think of a title.
4. Write your story on the page and illustrate it on the back.
5. Read your wacky story to a friend.

## Box 1

**Once there was**
- a big frog and a small worm
- a crab and a fish
- a dog with wings and a talking cat
- a pretty girl and a blue dragon

## Box 2

**who were**
- eating apples
- flying with a bird
- playing a game
- looking for a new friend

## Box 3

**Then**
- the clouds turned green
- a giant was seen
- a feather floated to the ground
- candy fell from the sky

## Box 4

**At last,**

You decide how your story will end.

_____
(Title)

By _____

**Once there was** _____

_____

**who were** _____

**Then** _____

_____

_____

_____

**At last,** _____

_____

_____

_____

**The End**

# Happy Holidays

Traditional family celebrations create warm memories of home. There's no better place to share this joyful unit.

## Joyful Reading

Unwrap this festive book collection to celebrate many different holiday seasons.
- *Celebrating* by Gwenyth Swain
- *Celebrations* by Myra Cohn Livingston
- *Celebrations of Light: A Year of Holidays Around the World* by Nancy Luenn

## Holiday Happenings

Celebrate the season as you choose from the following sparkling ideas.

| Skill—Activity | Title | Materials |
|---|---|---|
| Sorting—chart | "Holiday Circle" | copy of page 68, yearly calendar |
| Logical thinking—puzzle | "Basketful of Clues" | copy of pages 69 and 70 |
| Reading for details—booklet | "Light Up the Holidays" | copy of page 71, 2 sheets of black construction paper |
| Creative writing—story | "Imagine a Holiday" | copy of the top of page 72 |
| Following directions—game | "Hearts in the Right Place" | copy of the bottom of page 72, 4¹/₂" x 6" sheet of red construction paper, 4' sheet of white bulletin board paper |
| Following directions—graph | "Party Time!" | copy of page 73 |

## Extra Special Celebrations

- Spread festive cheer by including a holiday music cassette of your choice for each family to share. (A merry selection for the December holiday season is Hap Palmer's *Holiday Magic*.) Include a note to parents encouraging them to help their child memorize the words of one song and then perform it at a family gathering.

- Invite parents to help their child create a homemade card and gift for a loved one to encourage thoughtfulness and giving joy to others.

# Holiday Circle

**Parent note:** Invite your child to put his or her sorting skills to work with this activity. Have your child remove the calendar from the bag; then help your child read and follow the directions to complete this activity. If necessary, help your child use the calendar to determine in which season each holiday occurs.

## Directions:

1. Read each holiday.
2. Think about the season in which it occurs.
3. Write each holiday in the correct oval.
4. On the back of this sheet, draw a picture of your favorite holiday.

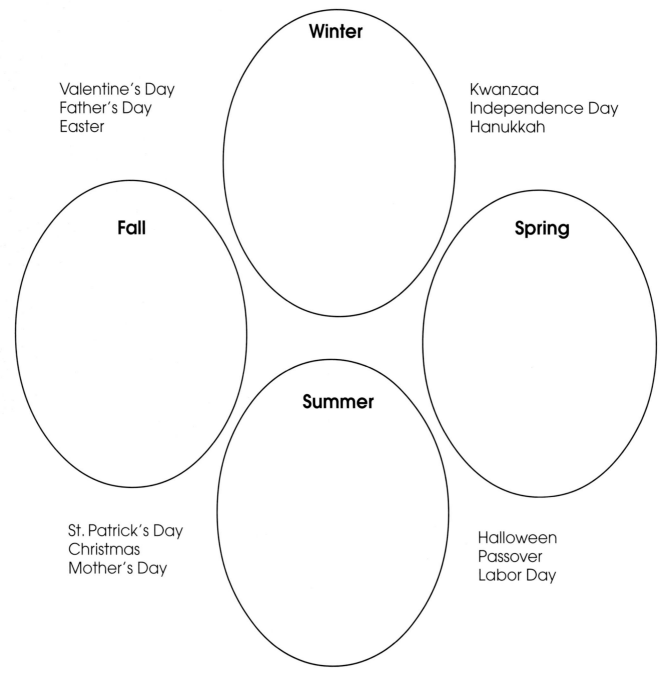

Valentine's Day
Father's Day
Easter

**Winter**

Kwanzaa
Independence Day
Hanukkah

**Fall**

**Spring**

**Summer**

St. Patrick's Day
Christmas
Mother's Day

Halloween
Passover
Labor Day

# Basketful of Clues

**Parent note:** Talk with your child about his or her favorite holiday symbols. Have your child remove the accompanying sheet from the bag. Then help your child read and follow the directions below to complete this puzzle. Encourage your child to explain the reason for each answer.

### Directions:

1. Cut out the holiday labels.
2. Look at the baskets on the next sheet.
   Match each label to a basket.
   Glue.
3. Read each clue.
4. Write each name on the correct tag.
5. Draw the item in the basket.

### Clues:

Jamal is sweet on candy. Add a toothbrush to his holiday basket.

Chocolate bunnies are Ashley's favorite! Add some colored eggs to her basket.

Emily picked some beautiful flowers for her mother. Add a ribbon to her basket.

It's picnic time! Alex can't wait to see the fireworks. Add a flag to his basket.

Gobble, gobble! Sam has filled his basket with a bird's favorite snack. Add a turkey to his basket.

| Thanksgiving | Mother's Day |
| Valentine's Day | Easter |
| Independence Day | |

# Holiday Baskets

# Light Up the Holidays

**Parent note:** Talk with your child about any holidays your family celebrates in December. Then help him or her understand that many families celebrate different holidays. Next, have your child remove the two sheets of construction paper from the bag. Read each holiday description to your child. Help your child read and follow the directions to make a booklet.

**Directions:**

1. Fold the two sheets of construction paper in half. Staple them together on the left side.
2. Cut out the title.
   Glue it on the cover.
3. Cut out the patterns and word boxes. Match one pattern with each word box.
4. Glue one pair on each page.
5. Decorate the booklet.

## Light Up the Holidays

Red, green, and black are the colors of **Kwanzaa.** The seven candles of the *kinara* represent the seven beliefs that are taught during this African American harvest festival.

In the Christian church, *Advent* candles are lit on each of the four Sundays before **Christmas.** The candles are arranged in a wreath of evergreen branches.

In Mexico, Las Posadas is celebrated on each of nine nights before Christmas Day. Luminaries called **farolitos** line the streets with candlelight.

Jewish people celebrate **Hanukkah,** or the Feast of Lights. Each *menorah* has nine candles. The center candle, or *shamash,* is used to light the other candles each night of the feast.

| **Advent wreath** | **menorah** | **kinara** | **farolito** |

# Imagine a Holiday

**Parent note:** Holidays are lots of fun! Help your child choose one of the pictures below to create a new holiday. Encourage your child to tell when, why, and how the holiday is celebrated. Encourage him or her to include special foods, decorations, and traditions. Invite your child to use the space below to plan. Then, on the back of this sheet, help him or her write a story describing the new holiday.

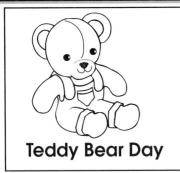

**Teddy Bear Day**

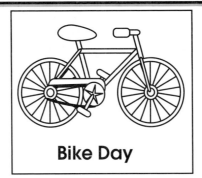

**Bike Day**

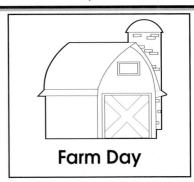

**Farm Day**

---

# Hearts in the Right Place

**Parent note:** This happy heart version of a favorite party game is just right for any holiday! Have your child remove the long paper and construction paper from the bag. Next, help your child read and follow the directions to make the game. To play, blindfold a family member, give her the heart shape and then spin her around three times. Encourage her to try to stick the heart in the correct place on the cutout. Invite each family member to take a turn.

### Directions:

1. Place the long paper flat on the floor.
2. Lie on it.
   Have someone trace your body.
3. Color your face and favorite clothes on it.
4. Cut it out.
5. Tape it to a door or wall.
6. Cut one heart shape from the red paper.
   Put tape on the back of it.
7. Play Hearts in the Right Place.

# Party Time!

**Parent note:** Help your child read and follow the directions below to complete the graph and answer the questions.

**Directions:**

1. Look at the graph.
2. Look at the picture. Count.
3. Color the bar graph.
4. Answer the questions.

Write.

Which has the fewest? _____

Which has the most? _____

| balloons | lights | cookies | party horns |
|----------|--------|---------|-------------|
| | | | |
| | | | |
| | | | |
| | | | |
| | | | |
| | | | |
| | | | |

73

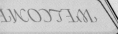

# Home, Sweet Home

There's no place like home for sharing love, laughter, and learning!

## Book Nook

Include several of these titles to encourage each youngster to snuggle up and read with a family member.

- *Animal Homes* by Betsey Chessen and Pamela Chanko
- *Homeplace* by Anne Shelby
- *A House for Hermit Crab* by Eric Carle
- *How a House Is Built* by Gail Gibbons
- *My Teacher Sleeps in School* by Leatie Weiss
- *The Three Little Wolves and the Big Bad Pig* by Eugene Trivizas
- *Town Mouse, Country Mouse* by Jan Brett

## Homeward Bound!

Send home some of these enriching activities to welcome parents into their child's learning.

| Skill—Activity | Title | Materials |
|---|---|---|
| Following directions—craft | "Homespun Love" | white construction paper copy of page 75, hole puncher, two 8" yarn lengths |
| Writing—booklet | "In My Home" | white construction paper copy of page 76, copy of page 77 |
| Oral language—song | "Homes All Around" | copy of the song on the top of page 78, copy of *Animal Homes* by Betsey Chessen and Pamela Chanko |
| Vocabulary—cooking | "Homemade Breakfast Treat" | copy of the recipe on the bottom of page 78 |
| Matching, writing—picture | "Build a House" | copy each of pages 79 and 80 |

## Door's Open!

- Send home a note encouraging parents to take their child on a nature walk to look for different types of animal homes, such as bird or squirrel nests.

- Encourage families to have a dinner-table discussion about what makes their home special. Is it love, people, photographs, pets, or something else?

# Homespun Love

**Parent note:** Talk to your child about what the saying written on the house means. Help your child read and follow the directions below to make this mobile. Encourage your child to add other elements, such as construction paper shutters or siding made from Popsicle sticks, to personalize the home. This special keepsake is a warm reminder of the love in your family.

### Directions:

1. Write your last name on the heart.

2. Color the heart and the house. Cut them out.

3. Punch a hole at each dot.

4. Tie a piece of yarn to the bottom of the house. Tie on the heart.

5. Make a yarn hanger for the house.

6. Hang your mobile.

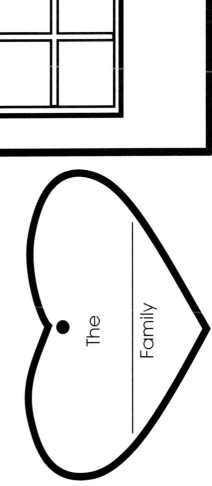

The _____
Family

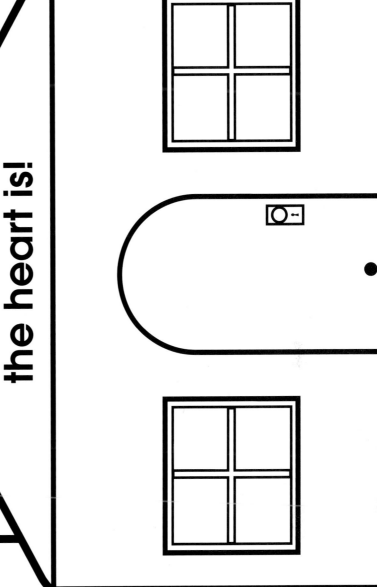

## Home is where the heart is!

75

# In My Home

**Parent note:** Home, sweet home! Invite your child to tell you what's special about his or her home. Have your child remove the accompanying sheet from the bag. Then help your child read and follow the directions below to make this unique booklet.

## Directions:

1. Look at the box on the house. Draw a picture of your family. Color the house.
2. Cut it out.
3. Cut out the booklet pages on the other sheet.
4. On each booklet page, finish the sentence. Also draw a picture.
5. Stack the pages in order. Staple them to the house.
6. Read your new book to someone in your family.

## In my home

you will see...
people who love and care for me!

Staple here.

5

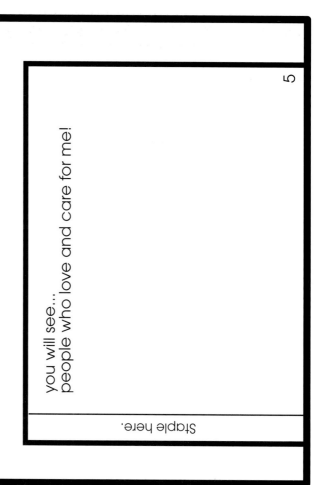

### Finished Sample

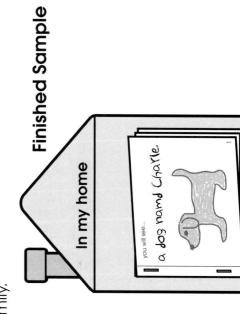

In my home

you will see...
a dog namd Charle.

| | |
|---|---|
| you will see… 2 | you will see… 4 |
| you will see… 1 | you will see… 3 |

# Homes All Around

**Parent note:** Help your child read *Animal Homes* by Betsey Chessen and Pamela Chanko and discuss the different types of homes. Then revisit the pages and sing the song below (to the tune of "The Wheels on the Bus") with your child.

A log is a home for a squirrel,
For a squirrel, for a squirrel.
A log is a home for a squirrel.
Home, sweet home!

A nest is a home for baby birds,
Baby birds, baby birds.
A nest is a home for baby birds.
Home, sweet home!

*Continue the song with other verses that match the book's illustrations.*

---

# Homemade Breakfast Treat

**Parent note:** Before beginning this cooking activity, talk about whole and half with your child. Then help your child read and follow the recipe, paying special attention to the boldfaced vocabulary words. Tips: Pick a relaxed morning to try this recipe. Prepare the toast and bacon in advance so they are cool enough for your child to safely handle. Have your child use a plastic knife (or butter knife) to carefully cut the ingredients. Then work together to assemble a house for each member of your family.

**Ingredients for one house:**
whole slice of French toast
$\frac{1}{2}$ slice of French toast, cut in a triangle shape
cooked bacon strip
whole strawberry
$\frac{1}{2}$ banana

**Utensils and supplies:**
plate
plastic knife (or butter knife)

**Directions:**

1. Put the whole piece of toast on your plate.
   This is the **house.**
2. Put the triangle of toast above the house.
   This is the **roof.**
3. Tear the strip of bacon in half.
   Use one half to make a door.
   Use the other half for a **chimney.**
4. Cut the strawberry in half.
   Use each half to make a **window.**
5. Cut the banana in slices.
   Use them to cover the roof.
6. Eat it up!

# Build a House

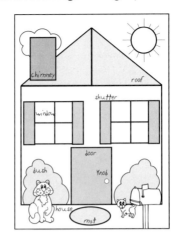

**Parent note:** Talk with your child about different types of homes, including houses, apartment buildings, and mobile homes. Encourage your child to think about the type of home you live in and how it looks. Then compare it with the house pictured at the right. Have your child remove the accompanying sheet from the bag. Help your child read and follow the directions below to build the pictured house.

## Directions:

1. Cut out the shapes.

2. Look at the picture of the house.

3. Look at the other sheet.
   Use the shapes to make the same house here.
   Glue them in place.

4. Color the house.

5. Label the parts of the house.

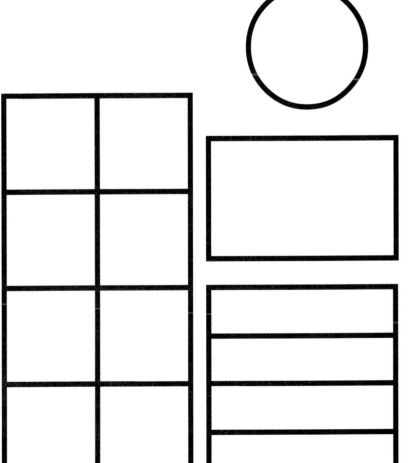

# Marvelous Mice

Scamper through this collection of mice-related activities and give your little ones something to squeak about!

### Mouse Tales

Include the following titles in the bag to encourage your youngsters to nibble on this assortment of mouse-filled literature.

- *Doctor DeSoto* by William Steig
- *Frederick* by Leo Lionni
- *If You Give a Mouse a Cookie* by Laura Joffe Numeroff
- *The Little Mouse, the Red Ripe Strawberry, and the Big Hungry Bear* by Audrey Wood
- *Whose Mouse Are You?* by Robert Kraus

### Merry Mice Fun

Send your little critters home with a "hole" lot of learning when you include a selection of these mouse-related activities.

| Skill—Activity | Title | Materials |
|---|---|---|
| Oral language—sorting | "As Small As a Mouse, As Large As a House" | copy of page 82, magazine, sheet of blank paper |
| Rhyming words—game | "A Game of Cat and Mouse" | gray construction paper copy of page 83, tan construction paper copy of page 84 |
| Rhyming words—rhyming clock | "Hickory, Dickory, Dock" | tagboard copy of page 85, brad |

### More Mouse Fun

- Include a note in the bag encouraging each family to play a game of Hide and Go Squeak. One family member is designated to be the cat and the others are the mice. The mice hide while the cat searches for them. When a mouse is found, he announces himself with a "Squeak!" He then helps the cat seek out the other mice.

# As Small As a Mouse, As Large As a House

**Parent note:** Here's a fun opportunity to help your child reinforce the concepts of large and small. Direct your child to remove the magazine from the bag. Next, help your child locate, cut out, and sort magazine pictures by large and small. Invite your youngster to talk about the differences in the pictures as he or she sorts and glues them to the chart below. If more space is needed, attach a blank sheet of paper to the bottom of the chart.

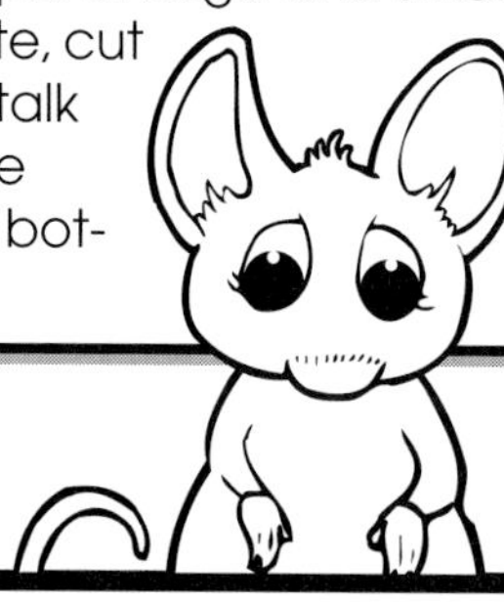

| Small | Large |
|-------|-------|
| 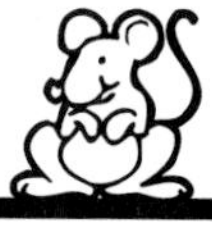       | 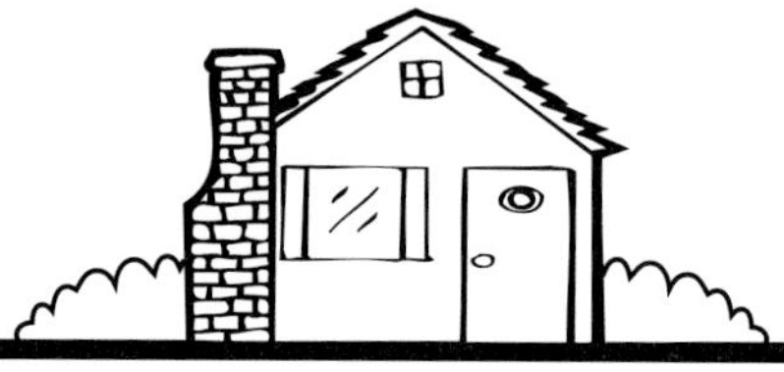       |
|       |       |

# A Game of Cat and Mouse

**Parent note:** Ask your child what makes words rhyme. Then have your child remove the accompanying sheet from the bag. Instruct your child to cut apart the game cards on both pages. Then help your child read and follow the directions to play this variation of a traditional memory game. For more reinforcement after the game, help your child think of additional rhyming words.

**Directions:**

1. Place the cards facedown.
   Mix them up.
   Spread them out.
2. Choose a gray card.
   Choose a tan card.
3. Read the word on each card.
4. If the words rhyme, keep the cards.
   If the words do not rhyme, return them to the game.

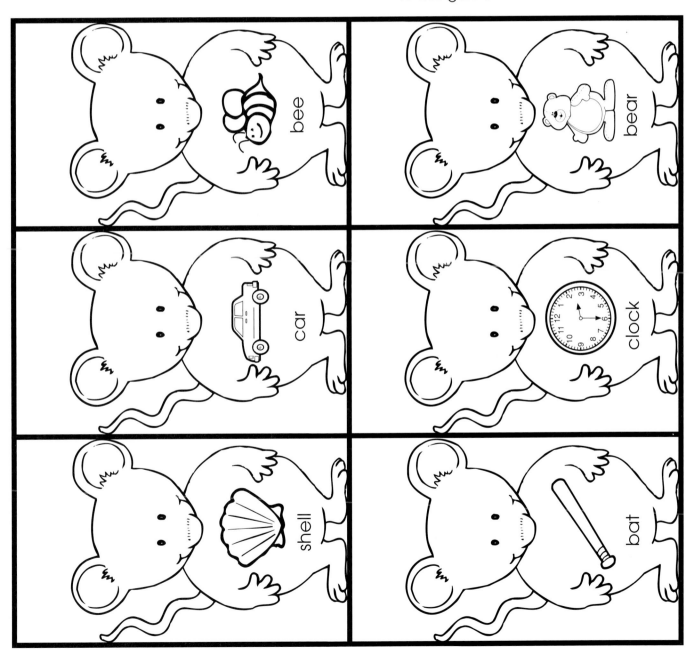

# Game Cards

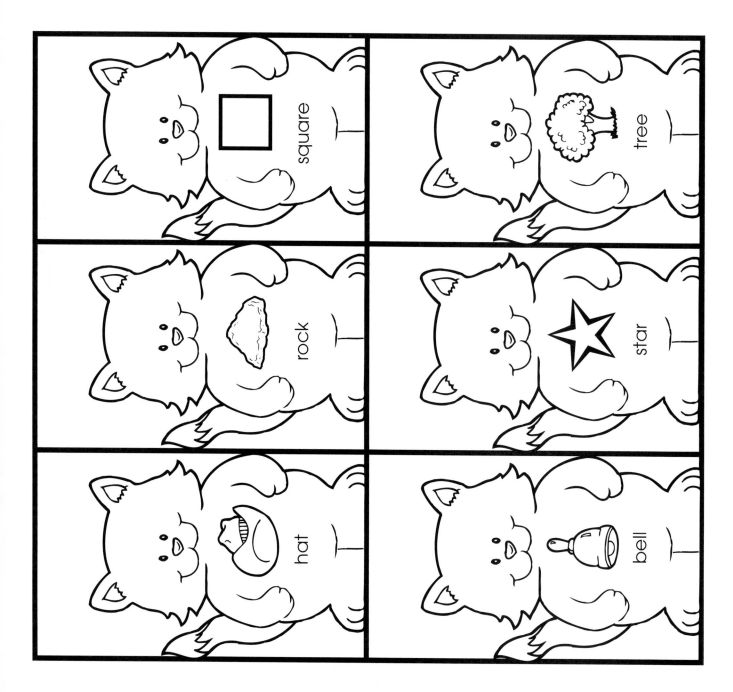

# Hickory, Dickory, Dock

**Parent note:** Make time for a rhyme by trying this variation of an old favorite! Help your child write a rhyming action word for as many clock numbers as possible. Next, have your child remove the brad from the bag. Direct your child to cut out the clockface and hands. Help your youngster attach the hands to the center of the clock with the brad. Encourage your youngster to repeat the rhyme below, each time replacing lines 3 and 4 with a different rhyming pair from the clock. Then have your child reset the clock to the new time.

> Hickory, dickory, dock,
> The mouse ran up the clock.
> The clock struck (<u>one</u>);
> The mouse (<u>did run</u>),
> Hickory, dickory, dock!

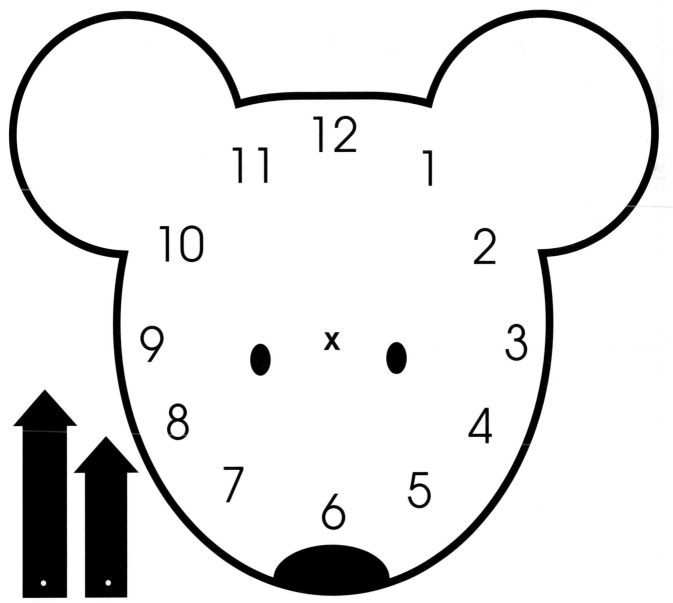

# See the Ocean!

Ahoy there, matey—it's high tide for learning! Invite your little sailors and their families to set sail with this ocean unit.

## Get Hooked on Books

What's the catch of the day? This selection of seaworthy literature, of course!

- *Harry by the Sea* by Gene Zion
- *Into the Sea* by Brenda Z. Guiberson
- *The Magic School Bus on the Ocean Floor* by Joanna Cole
- *My Life With the Wave* by Catherine Cowan
- *The Seashore Book* by Charlotte Zolotow
- *A Swim Through the Sea* by Kristin Joy Pratt

## Seaworthy Activities

Choose from these literacy-rich activities for a "sand-sational" take-home bag!

| Skill—Activity | Title | Materials |
|---|---|---|
| Classification—game | "Too Many Fish in the Sea" | copy of *A Swim Through the Sea*, white construction paper copy each of pages 87 and 88, 2 individual serving-size bags of fish-shaped crackers, paper lunch bag |
| Creative writing—story starter | "If I Went Out to Sea" | copy of page 89 |
| Oral language—song | "Old Man Skipper" | copy of page 90 |
| Vocabulary—cooking | "Seaworthy Dessert" | copy of page 91 |

## Blue Wave Specials

- For more imaginary sea adventures, include a note encouraging parents to use the following directions to make a water globe with their child. To make one, half-fill a baby food jar with lightly tinted water; then add some sand and a few small seashells. Glue the lid on. When the glue is dry, shake the globe for waves of fun!

- Enclose a sheet of drawing paper, a small resealable bag of sand, and a note inviting family members to draw themselves at the beach. Ask them to glue sand to the bottom of the paper for a beachy touch after they color the picture.

# Too Many Fish in the Sea

**Parent note:** Reread a nonfiction book about oceans, such as *A Swim Through the Sea*, and point out the different types of ocean animals. Together, look at the cards below and say the animal names. Next, have your child remove the accompanying page from the bag. Invite your child to cut out the gameboards and the cards and then give one board to his or her partner. Guide your child and his or her partner in coloring each animal on their boards to match the cards. Ask your child to remove the paper bag and fish-shaped crackers from the bag; then help your child read and follow the directions below to play the game.

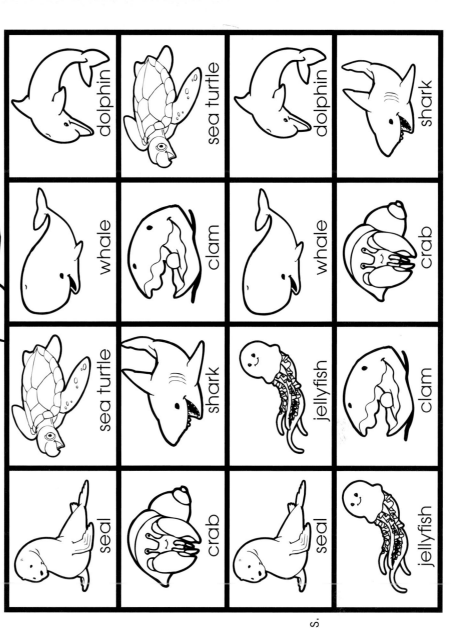

| | | | |
|---|---|---|---|
| seal | sea turtle | whale | dolphin |
| crab | shark | clam | sea turtle |
| seal | jellyfish | whale | dolphin |
| jellyfish | clam | crab | shark |

## Directions:

1. Put the cards in the paper bag. Give each player a bag of fish crackers.

2. Pick a card from the paper bag.

3. Read the card. Show the picture.

4. Look at your gameboard. If you have a match, put a fish on top of it. If there is not a match, do nothing.

5. Pick another card and repeat. The first player to cover three boxes in a row wins.

6. Put the cards back in the bag. Play again.

7. When the game is over, eat your fish!

| | | | |
|---|---|---|---|
| seal | sea turtle | whale | dolphin |
| crab | shark | clam | sea turtle |
| jellyfish | clam | crab | whale |
| shark | dolphin | seal | jellyfish |

| | | | |
|---|---|---|---|
| shark | whale | clam | seal |
| clam | seal | shark | dolphin |
| jellyfish | sea turtle | crab | whale |
| crab | dolphin | jellyfish | sea turtle |

**Skill:** *Creative writing—story starter*

**Parent note:** Talk with your child about what he or she might see on an ocean outing. Encourage your child to consider ocean animals such as fish and birds, and objects such as boats, buoys, and lighthouses. Then help your child read, complete, and illustrate the story starter below.

# If I went out to sea, I might see...

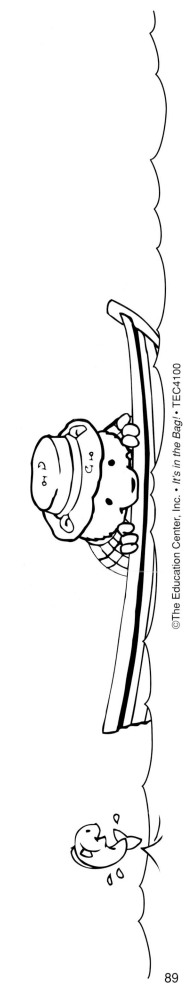

**Parent note:** What do you see at sea? Old Man Skipper sees quite a lot! Help your child read and sing the chorus and verse of the song below. Encourage him or her to act out the ocean animal's movement as the song is sung. Then help your child substitute a different ocean animal and movement pair for the next verse. Invite your child to create more ocean animal and movement pairs. Continue singing and substituting as long as desired.

# Old Man Skipper

*(sung to the tune of "Old MacDonald Had a Farm")*

Chorus: Old Man Skipper sailed the sea
To see what he could see.

And in that sea he saw
(A whale) swimming happily!
With a (swoosh, swoosh) here,
And a (swoosh, swoosh) there.
Here a (swoosh), there a (swoosh),
Everywhere a (swoosh, swoosh)!

*Repeat the chorus.*

More ocean animal and movement pairs:
An eel; wiggle, wiggle
A dolphin; flip, flip
A shark; splash, splash
A crab; pinch, pinch
A seal; bark, bark

# Seaworthy Dessert

**Parent note:** Shiver me timbers—it's time for a treat! Invite your child to help you make this delicious dessert to wind up your ocean study. Follow the directions printed on the box to make a clear bowlful of blue gelatin, encouraging your child to observe. Halfway through the chilling time, invite your child to put some candy fish into the "ocean." When the gelatin ocean is set, help your child read and follow the directions below to complete the seaworthy dessert.

**Ingredients:**
box blue gelatin mix (to represent the ocean)
Swedish or Gummy fish
Cool Whip Squeeze whipped topping
fruit roll

**Utensils and supplies:**
clear bowl
plastic knife
toothpicks
individual serving bowls
spoons

## Directions:

1. **Cut** the fruit roll into four squares.

2. Cut each square into two triangles.

3. Make a sailboat.
   Roll one triangle as shown (boat).
   Put a triangle on a toothpick (sail).
   **Put** the toothpick mast into the **boat** bottom.

4. Make more sailboats.

5. Take the ocean out of the refrigerator.
   **Ask** for help if you need it.

6. Get the whipped topping.
   Squeeze some waves onto the ocean.

7. Float the sailboats on the **ocean.**

8. Scoop some ocean into a bowl.
   Eat!

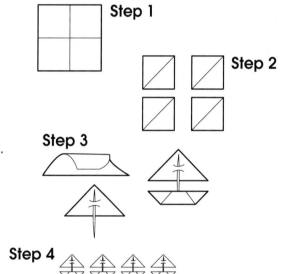

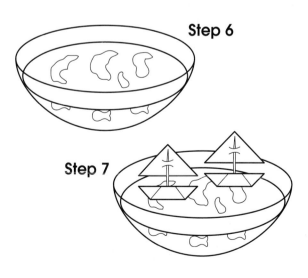

# Hooray for 100!

...97, 98, 99, 100! Spotlight the number 100 with an exciting bag that's sure to provide fun for the whole family on the 100th day of school, or any day of the year!

## Books You Can Count On

Youngsters will eagerly count along with a selection of these 100-related books.
- *Emily's First 100 Days of School* by Rosemary Wells
- *From One to One Hundred* by Teri Sloat
- *One Hundred Hungry Ants* by Elinor J. Pinczes
- *100th Day Worries* by Margery Cuyler
- *The Wolf's Chicken Stew* by Keiko Kasza

### Here's to 100

Just a few of these activities will add up to a stronger understanding of the concept of 100.

| Skill—Activity | Title | Materials |
|---|---|---|
| Creative writing—stories | "Story Starters for 100" | copy of page 93, envelope |
| Writing—lists | "100 Wonderful Things" | copy of page 94, 5 sheets of different-colored construction paper |
| Following directions—movement | "100% Fun" | copy of page 95, paper lunch bag |
| Oral language—craft making | "100-Year-Old Art" | copy of the top of page 96, silhouette (cut from a 12" x 18" sheet of tan or other skin-toned construction paper as shown below), sheet of 12" x 18" construction paper, craft items |
| Comprehension—counting activity | "Know the Rows" | copy of *One Hundred Hungry Ants,* copy of the bottom of page 96, copy of page 97, 100 plastic ant counters (optional) |

### All Together Now

- Send a note home encouraging each family to decide on a project that includes the number 100, such as reading 100 books over a set period of time or collecting 100 items of a particular type.

# Story Starters for 100

**Parent note:** Ask your child to think about how much 100 of something can be. Then use this activity to help him or her share these thoughts. Help your child read and complete each story starter below. Have your child cut the story starters apart and then store them in the envelope provided. Then have one family member draw a story starter from the envelope and then begin to write a funny story. After she has written a sentence or two, encourage her to pass it to the next member. When each member has taken a turn, return the story to the first writer, who will create an ending sentence. Invite a family member to read the completed story aloud. If desired, have a different family member begin to write a new story the next day.

I wish I had **100** _____.

I can eat **100** _____.

I can carry **100** _____.

I would buy _____ with **100** dollars.

I would like to give my friend **100** _____.

I would like to collect **100** _____.

In **100** years, I hope there will be _____.

I would not want **100** _____.

# 100 Wonderful Things

**Parent note:** Use this five-day activity to show your child how he or she can count to 100! Have your child remove the construction paper from the bag. Next, help your child cut out the pictures below and glue each onto a separate sheet of paper. On the first day, help your child read the topic on a picture and make the list. Continue in this manner each day until all the lists are complete. After writing, count along with your child to make sure that 100 things are listed. If desired, glue the edges of the lists together to create a large poster. Wow—100!

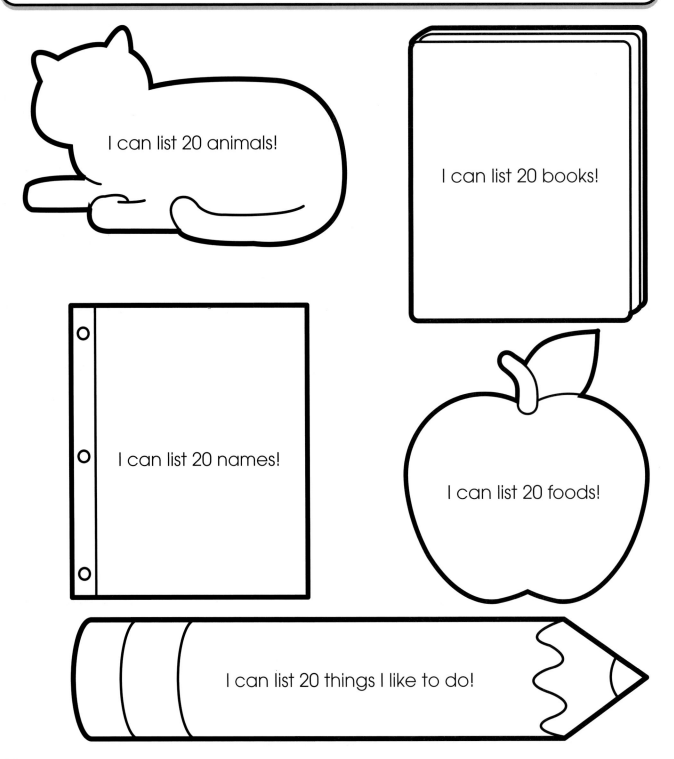

I can list 20 animals!

I can list 20 books!

I can list 20 names!

I can list 20 foods!

I can list 20 things I like to do!

# 100% Fun

**Parent note:** This activity will really get your family moving and grooving! Have your child remove the paper lunch sack from the bag. Help him or her follow the directions to prepare the movement activities. Continue to complete one activity each day for several days. "98, 99, 100!"

## Directions:

1. Cut the cards apart. Put them in the bag.
2. Draw a card each day. Read it.
3. Complete the activity with your family.

 Run for 100 seconds.

Take a 100-step walk.

Jump 100 times.

 Dance for 100 seconds.

 Bounce a ball 100 times.

Do 100 jumping jacks.

Stand on one foot for 100 seconds.

 Brush your teeth for 100 seconds.

 Eat 100 cereal pieces.

Count 100 objects.

# 100-Year-Old Art

**Parent note:** Ask your child what his or her appearance will be at age 100. Will he or she have wrinkles? Gray hair? A happy smile? What will his or her life be like? Then prepare for this self-portrait activity by having your child remove the paper silhouette cutout, sheet of construction paper, and craft items from the bag. Provide assistance as your child reads and follows the directions below to complete the portrait. Bet this self-portrait will provide an interesting glimpse into the future!

### Directions:

1. Look at the cutout.
   Draw your 100-year-old face.
2. Crumple the cutout to add wrinkles.
   Smooth it out.
3. Glue the cutout to the construction paper.
4. Use crayons and craft items to complete your picture.
5. Write your name.
6. Tell what it is like to be 100 years old.

©The Education Center, Inc. • *It's in the Bag!* • TEC4100

- - - - - - - - - - - - - - - - - - - - - - - - - - - - - - - - - - - - - -

Skill: *Comprehension—counting activity*

# Know the Rows

**Parent note:** Take a few minutes to read and discuss the book *One Hundred Hungry Ants* with your child. Focus on the ways the ants line up in rows equaling 100, and help your child count along with the pictures. Then have your child remove the accompanying sheet from the bag. Help him or her cut apart the ant patterns and then revisit the pages where the ants are lined up in one row of 100. Invite your child to line up his or her ants in the same fashion. Repeat with different methods of counting (two rows of 50, four rows of 25, etc.). "A hey and a hi dee ho!"

©The Education Center, Inc. • *It's in the Bag!* • TEC4100

# Pass the Peanuts!

It's no secret: Peanuts are popular! So pack a bagful of fresh peanut ideas for youngsters and their families to bite into.

## Harvest a Crop

Mmmm—these books provide a hearty helping of peanutty fact and fiction. Enjoy!

- *From Peanuts to Peanut Butter* by Melvin Berger
- *The Life and Times of the Peanut* by Charles Micucci
- *Peanut Butter and Jelly: A Play Rhyme* illustrated by Nadine Bernard Westcott
- *What's for Lunch? Peanuts* by Claire Llewellyn

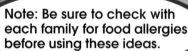

**Note: Be sure to check with each family for food allergies before using these ideas.**

## Fresh-Roasted Activities

Enjoy a selection of tasteful activities based on our favorite legume!

| Skill—Activity | Title | Materials |
|---|---|---|
| Descriptive words—poem | "Peanutty Poetry" | copy of page 99, roasted-in-the-shell peanut |
| Comprehension, vocabulary—diagram | "Peanut Plant Pizzazz" | nonfiction book about peanuts, such as *What's for Lunch? Peanuts*, copy of page 100 |
| Observation, prediction—game | "Peanut Mystery Mastery" | resealable plastic bag containing 20 roasted-in-the-shell peanuts, copy of page 101 |
| Vocabulary, fine motor—cooking | "Peanut Butter Play Dough" | copy of page 102 |
| Creative writing—booklet | "The Best Peanut Butter Sandwich" | white construction paper copy of page 103, five 6" squares of white construction paper |

## Goober Goodies

- Send home a note encouraging families to take this special snack along on their next outing. For each serving, combine one tablespoon each of these high-energy foods in a small reseaable plastic bag: roasted peanuts, raisins, cereal pieces, and chocolate chips. Seal, shake, and snack!

- Include a note inviting families to play the Popular Peanut game! On a trip to the grocery store, encourage families to notice as many peanut foods as possible. Encourage older students to extend their search to include other items made with peanuts, such as facial cream, cat litter, paint, and soap.

# Peanutty Poetry

**Parent note:** Invite your child to remove the peanut from the bag. Encourage him or her to explore the peanut by sight, touch, smell, sound, and taste. Help your child brainstorm a list of words that describe the peanut. Then help your child read and follow the directions below to write an original shape poem about peanuts. Sounds delicious!

## Directions:

1. Read your word list.

2. Look at the peanut shape below. Write the word peanut.

3. Write a poem. Write words from your list. Write each word around the shape.

4. Read your poem.

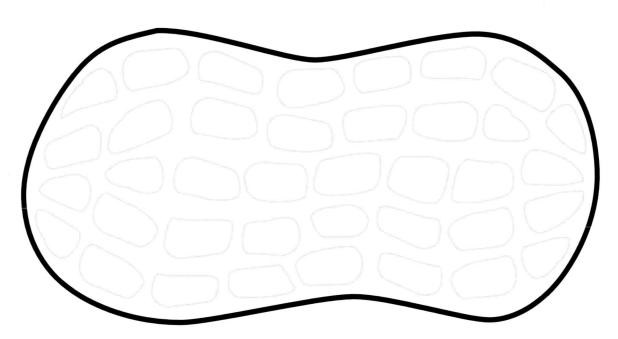

# Peanut Plant Pizzazz

Peanuts are **seeds.** They grow in **pods** underground. The plant grows **flowers** that grow long **pegs.** The pegs grow down into the soil. The peg ends turn into pods. Seeds grow in the pods. The farmer harvests the pods and dries them. He will keep some seeds to plant next year.

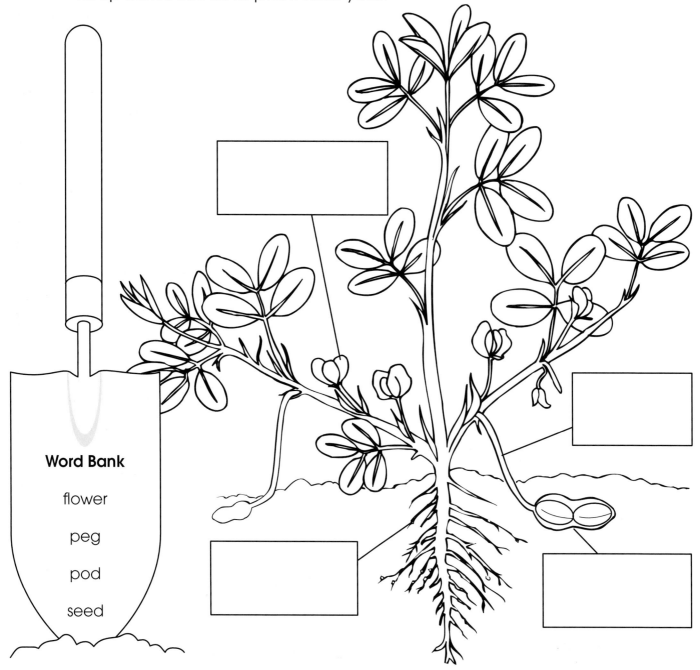

**Word Bank**

flower

peg

pod

seed

©The Education Center, Inc. • *It's in the Bag!* • TEC4100

# Peanut Mystery Mastery

**Parent note:** Have your child remove the peanuts from the bag. Invite him or her to examine a few and to notice the different shapes and sizes of the shells. Tell your child that peanut pods (or shells) don't always have the same amount of seeds inside; they can have one, two, or even three or more! Next, direct your child to cut out the gameboards. Have each partner take one gameboard and eight peanuts (there are extras in the bag in case any are broken). Then help your child read and follow the directions below to play the game.

## Directions:

1. Pick a peanut.
   Look at it.

2. How many peanut seeds are inside?
   Predict.

3. Look at the first square on your gameboard.
   Write your guess.

4. Trade peanuts with your partner.
   Open your partner's peanut shell.

5. Check the seeds.
   Partners tell each other how many seeds there are.

6. Look at your gameboard again.
   Write how many.

7. Compare.

8. Play again!

9. When you and your partner have opened all the shells, the game is over.
   Count how many times you were right.

| Predict | Predict | Predict | Predict |
|---------|---------|---------|---------|
| Check | Check | Check | Check |
| Predict | Predict | Predict | Predict |
| Check | Check | Check | Check |

| Predict | Predict | Predict | Predict |
|---------|---------|---------|---------|
| Check | Check | Check | Check |
| Predict | Predict | Predict | Predict |
| Check | Check | Check | Check |

# Peanut Butter Play Dough

**Parent note:** This dough is both fun to play with and a nutritious treat! Clean a plastic placemat or work surface thoroughly; then help your child read and follow the directions below to make peanut butter play dough. While reading, help your child pay special attention to the boldfaced vocabulary words, and discuss each spelling and meaning. Store any leftover dough in an airtight container in the refrigerator for two to three days.

**Ingredients:**
$1/4$ c. creamy peanut butter
$1/4$ c. honey
$1$–$1 1/4$ c. dry milk powder

**Utensils and supplies:**
mixing bowl
spoon

## Directions:

1. Put the ingredients in the bowl.

2. **Stir** them together.

3. Use your **hands** to mix.
   If it is too sticky, add more **milk** powder.

4. Work with the **dough.**
   Make letters.
   Make words.
   Have **fun.**

5. Eat some!

# The Best Peanut Butter Sandwich

**Parent note:** Here are a couple of nifty facts to share with your child: More than half the peanuts grown in the United States are made into peanut butter. Americans eat more than 800 million pounds of peanut butter every year! In honor of this very popular spread, ask your child to brainstorm some possible sandwich combinations. Have your child remove the paper from the bag. Then direct him or her to cut out the text strips below. Help your child staple the pages to make a booklet. Assist him or her in titling the cover and gluing one text strip to each page. Then help your child read and follow the directions below to make the wild and wacky sandwiches!

## Directions:

1. Open the booklet to page 1.
   Read the words.

2. Think of a descriptive word to go in the first blank.
   Write it.

3. Think of a food to go in the second blank.
   Write it.

4. Read your sentence.

5. Draw a picture of it.

6. Turn the page.

7. Repeat the steps until all the pages are done.

8. Decorate the cover.

The _____ sandwich is peanut butter and _____.

The _____ sandwich is peanut butter and _____.

The _____ sandwich is peanut butter and _____.

The _____ sandwich is peanut butter and _____.

# A Child's Best Friend

No bones about it, your youngsters and their families will give this activity bag two paws-up!

### "Paws-itively" Great Books

Come. Sit. Read! Enjoy a selection of these books.

- *Franklin Wants a Pet* by Paulette Bourgeois
- *John Willy and Freddy McGee* by Holly Meade
- *Millions of Cats* by Wanda Ga'g
- *Pet Show!* by Ezra Jack Keats
- *Six-Dinner Sid* by Inga Moore

## Pet Essentials

Choose from the following pet-related activities to build a "s-s-super" take-home bag.

| Skill—Activity | Title | Materials |
|---|---|---|
| Creative writing—journal | "My Pet Journal" | copy of page 105 and enough copies of page 106 to make a desired number of journal pages |
| Observation—recording information | "Pet Detective" | copy of page 107 |
| Reading number words—game | "Pet Parade" | copy of page 108 |
| Following directions—puppets | "Presenting Pet Puppets" | white construction paper copy of page 109 |
| Following directions—sorting | "All Sorts of Pets" | copy of page 110 |

### Kennel Up

- For added interest, tuck a class pet (a small stuffed animal) and a spiral-bound notebook in the bag. Include a note asking family members to use their imaginations to write about the adventures of the class pet in their home. Encourage each family to share the pet's adventures for some "purr-fect" reading fun!

- Include some drawing paper and a note asking the student to create and draw an imaginary pet and write a short description of it. Wonder what fanciful creatures your youngsters will dream of?

Skill: *Creative writing—journal*

# My Pet Journal

**Parent note:** If you have a pet, talk about it with your child. If you don't have a pet, ask your child to imagine what kind of pet would be best to have. Help your child complete the front and back covers (below) and cut them out. Ask your child to remove the accompanying sheets from the bag. Help him or her assemble the journal by cutting apart the daily journal pages and then stapling them between the covers. Encourage your youngster to write (and illustrate on the facing page) a daily journal entry about a very special pet—real or imaginary.

(Front cover—staple here.)

## My Pet Journal

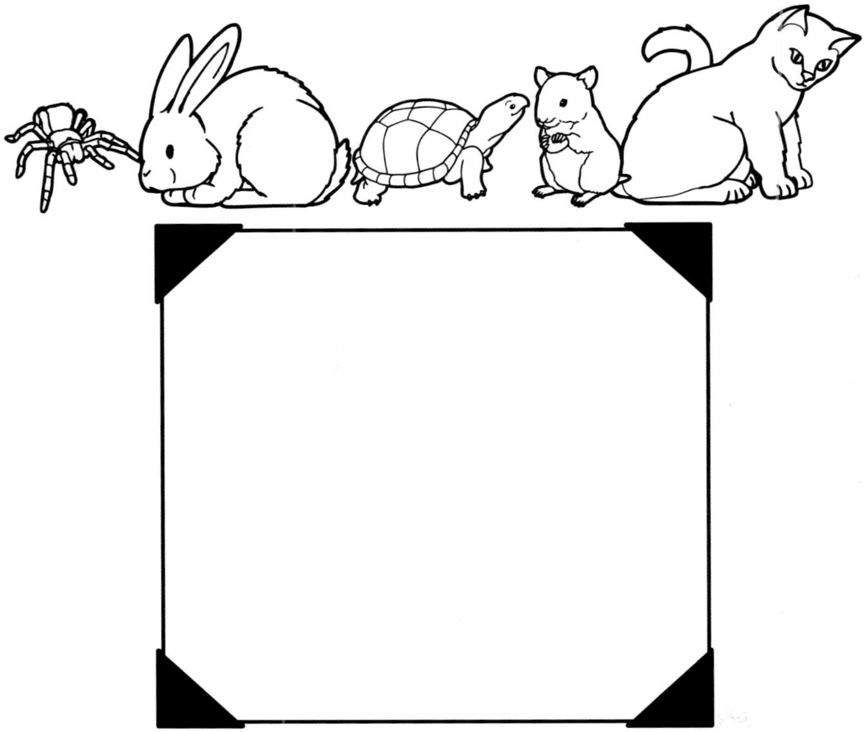

by ____________________



All About ____________________

(name)

My pet is ____________________.

My pet is ____________________ old.

My pet eats ____________________.

My pet is special because

____________________

____________________

____________________

____________________.

# Today is
— Sunday
— Monday
— Tuesday
— Wednesday
— Thursday
— Friday
— Saturday

# I cared for my pet by

_____

_____

_____

# Today is
— Sunday
— Monday
— Tuesday
— Wednesday
— Thursday
— Friday
— Saturday

# I cared for my pet by

_____

_____

_____

# Pet Detective

**Parent note:** This pet detective activity is just right to help strengthen observation skills. Help your child gather information about his or her pet and then read and complete each sentence below. If your child doesn't own a pet, have him choose a favorite stuffed animal or think of a make-believe pet and then complete the sentences.

My pet is smaller than _____.

My pet is larger than _____.

My pet weighs less than _____.

My pet weighs more than _____.

My pet is about the same size as _____.

My pet sleeps about _____ hours each day.

My pet plays about _____ minutes each day.

My pet eats for about _____ minutes each day.

My pet exercises about _____ minutes each day.

My pet does _____ most of the time.

# Pet Parade

**Parent note:** Everybody loves a parade—even pets! To play this partner game, have your child cut apart the picture cards along the bold lines, shuffle them, and place them facedown on a table. In turn, each player selects a card and reads the number word. The player folds the card along the dotted lines and then stands it upright, placing it in the correct order. Play continues until each card has been placed.

**Directions:**

1. Choose a card.
2. Read the number word.
3. Put the card in the correct order.

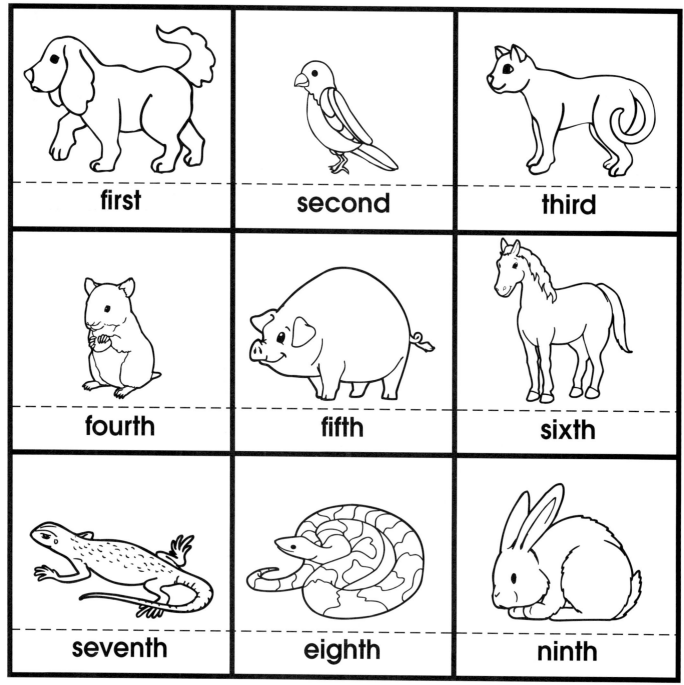

| first | second | third |
| fourth | fifth | sixth |
| seventh | eighth | ninth |

# Presenting Pet Puppets

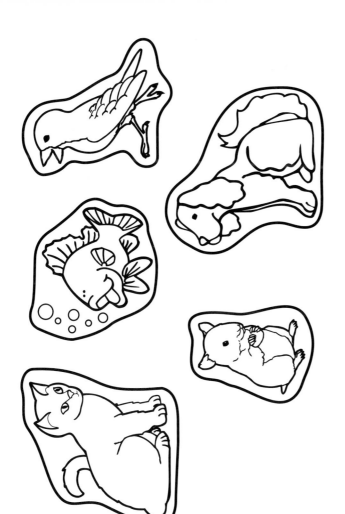

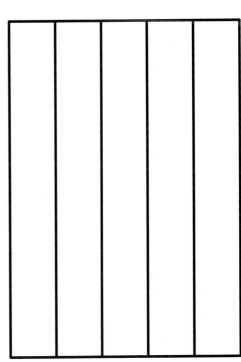

**Parent note:** These friendly puppets will encourage some creative language play. Help your child read and follow the directions below to make finger puppets. In Steps 3 and 4, your child may need extra help cutting the strips to the appropriate lengths and making the puppets. For more fun, put on a puppet or two yourself and join in the play. Bravo!

## Directions:

1. Color each pet.

2. Cut out the pets and strips.

3. Wrap a strip around your finger. Ask someone to tape it to make a ring. Take off the ring.

4. Tape a pet to the ring.

5. Repeat Steps 3 and 4 for each pet.

6. Put on the pet puppets.

7. Use your pet puppets to act out a play.

# All Sorts of Pets

**Parent note:** Talk with your child about the different characteristics of good pets and what kinds of animals make good pets. Then help your child read and follow the directions below. After your child sorts the cards as suggested in Step 3, have him or her think of other ways to sort the cards.

### Directions:

1. Color each animal.
2. Cut apart the cards.
3. Sort the cards by these rules:

- Fur and no fur
- Wings and no wings

- Legs, two legs, and no legs
- Pets and not pets

# Plenty of Pigs!

Pudgy, pink, and fun galore—these piggy ideas will have youngsters oinking for more!

### Pig Tales

Pack your bag with this "a-snort-ment" of books for families to root through.

- *All Pigs Are Beautiful* by Dick King-Smith
- *If You Give a Pig a Pancake* by Laura Joffe Numeroff
- *Pigs Aplenty, Pigs Galore!* by David McPhail
- *Piggies* by Audrey and Don Wood
- *Poppleton* by Cynthia Rylant
- *The True Story of the 3 Little Pigs* by John Scieszka

### Piggy Picks

Your youngsters will go hog-wild over these pig-related activities!

| Skill—Activity | Title | Materials |
|---|---|---|
| Writing—booklet | "This Little Piggy" | copy of pages 112 and 113, one 10" yarn length, stapler |
| Rhyming words—fingerplay | "Five Little Piglets" | copy of the poem on page 114 |
| Vocabulary—cooking | "Positively Perfect Pancakes" | copy of the recipe on page 115 |
| Following directions—piggy bank | "Pennies and Pigs" | pink construction paper copy of page 116 |

### More to Squeal About

- Enclose two pink party cups and four feet of pink yarn with a note inviting parents and children to make a pair of pig snouts for dramatic play. Be sure to include the following directions: To make one, draw nostrils on the bottom of a cup. Next, punch two holes, opposite one another, near the rim of the cup. Then tie a piece of yarn to each hole. Watch out, Big Bad Wolf!
- Picnics are perfect places to reinforce early phonics skills! Send home a note encouraging parents to pack foods whose names start with the letter *P,* such as peanut butter, potato salad, pickles, and peaches. Then suggest they take their children to pig out. Where? The park, of course!

# This Little Piggy

## Directions:

1. Write your name on the front cover.
   Color the pig.

2. Look at booklet page 1.

3. Read the sentence.
   Write an ending for it.
   Draw a picture of it.
   Do not draw the pig.

4. Repeat Step 3 for the rest of the booklet pages.

5. Read your booklet.
   Use the pig to help you tell the story.

# This Little Piggy

by _____

©The Education Center, Inc.

This little piggy

_____
(action)

2

This little piggy went

_____
(place)

1

And this little piggy went,
"Wee, wee, wee!" all the way

_____
(place)

5

This little piggy had

_____
(food)

4

This little piggy ate

_____
(food)

3

©The Education Center, Inc. • *It's in the Bag!* • TEC4100

# Five Little Piglets

(Five) little piglets rolling in the pen.

*(Hold up (five) fingers. Then make a rolling motion with both hands.)*

One ran away from Farmer Ben.

*(Hold up one finger; then hide it behind your back.)*

The horse told the cow, and the cow told the hen.

*(Cup one hand around mouth as if telling a secret and turn head to spread the news.)*

"Oink, oink!" went the piglets. And then…

*(Make snorting noises for the "oinks" and cover mouth with hand as if trying to hide laughter.)*

*Continue counting down until one piglet is left; then chant this last verse:*

One little piglet rolling in the pen.

*(Hold up one finger. Then make a rolling motion with both hands.)*

He ran away from Farmer Ben.

*(Hold up one finger; then hide it behind your back.)*

The horse told the cow, and the cow told the hen.

*(Cup one hand around mouth as if telling a secret and turn head to spread the news.)*

Then *all* the little piglets came back to their pen,

*(Wiggle fingers on one hand.)*

As Farmer Ben yelled, "Don't do that again!"

*(Shake pointer finger to scold.)*

# Positively Perfect Pancakes

**Parent note:** If you give a family a recipe, they'll make pancakes for breakfast! Read *If You Give a Pig a Pancake* with your child. Then ask him or her to predict what will happen when the pig finally gets her pancakes at the end of the story. Next, using your favorite pancake recipe, make one large and one small pancake for each person in your family, letting your child help as appropriate. Paying special attention to the boldfaced vocabulary words, help your child read and follow the recipe below to make a pig for each member of your family.

**Ingredients for four:**
4 large pancakes
4 small pancakes
12 banana slices
8 raisins
Cool Whip Squeeze whipped topping
   (or squeezable frosting)
syrup (to represent mud)

**Utensils and supplies:**
4 plates
4 forks
plastic knife

**Directions to make one:**

1. Put a large **pancake** on your plate.
2. Put a **small** pancake on **top** of the large one.
3. Make two ears and one nose with banana slices.
4. Add two raisin eyes.
5. Make a tail, mouth, and **legs** with the whipped cream (or frosting).
6. Cover the pig with **mud.**
7. Pig out!

# Pennies and Pigs

**Parent note:** What's the best kind of bank? The piggy bank, of course! Talk with your child about saving money and good places to keep it. Next, wash out a plastic, half-gallon milk jug. After it dries, put the lid on. Use a craft knife to cut a money slot along the edge of the jug that's on the opposite side of the handle as shown. Then help your child read and follow the directions below to make a piggy bank.

## Directions:

1. Cut out the pig parts below.
2. Glue the snout to the jug lid.
3. Glue the eyes to the jug above the snout.
4. Fold the ears on the dotted lines.
   Glue them to the jug.
5. Glue the legs to the jug.
6. Wrap the tail around a pencil to curl it.
   Glue it to the jug.
7. Put your money in the piggy bank.
8. What will you save your money for?
   Write about it on the back of this sheet.

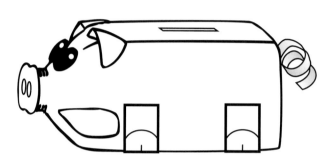

©The Education Center, Inc. • *It's in the Bag!* • TEC4100

Fold here.

Fold here.

# Pizza Pizzazz!

Think gooey cheese. Think scrumptious toppings. Think appetizing literacy-based activities for students and families! That's right—this literature unit about the popular pizza pie is perfect for home delivery!

## Start With a Great Base

The perfect pizza begins with a great crust. Begin your perfect pizza unit by placing a selection of these pizza-related books in the bag.

- *Curious George and the Pizza* by Margret and H. A. Rey
- *Hold the Anchovies! A Book About Pizza* by Shelley Rotner and Julia Pemberton Hellums
- *Little Nino's Pizzeria* by Karen Barbour

## Preferred Pizza Ingredients
Add a variety of these activities for a real pizza treat!

| Skill—Activity | Title | Materials |
|---|---|---|
| Letter sounds, vocabulary—puzzle | "Double *Z* Word Mystery" | copy of pages 118 and 119 |
| Descriptive words, nouns—poem | "Pizza Poetry" | copy of page 120 |
| Beginning letters—game | "Can You Top This?" | copy of page 121, die programmed with the letters *P, P, I, Z, A,* and *E.* |
| Vocabulary—puzzle | "A Tricky Pizza Puzzle" | copy of page 122 |

## Special Toppings

- Suggest that the family visit a local pizza parlor that allows customers to watch their pizza being prepared.
- Enclose a recording of Charlotte Diamond's song "I Am a Pizza."

# Double Z Word Mystery

**Parent note:** *Pizza* isn't the only word with a double *z*. Help your child read each word in the word bank below. Then have your child remove the accompanying sheet from the bag. Help your child read and follow the directions below to solve each word mystery.

## Directions:

1. Read the riddles below.

2. Read the word bank. Match each riddle to a word in the word bank.

3. Look at the next sheet. Write each word on the crust of a different pizza slice.

4. Draw a picture of each word.

### Word Bank

| | |
|---|---|
| buzz | fizz |
| pizza | drizzle |
| jazz | grizzly |
| blizzard | sizzle |

1. I am a crust with tomato sauce, pepperoni, and cheese.
   What am I? ___ ___ z z ___

2. I am a big bear.
   What am I? ___ ___ ___ z z ___ ___

3. This is a cool kind of music.
   What is it? ___ ___ z z

4. This is a big snowstorm.
   What is it? ___ ___ ___ z z ___ ___ ___

5. This is the sound of bacon frying.
   What is it? ___ ___ z z ___ ___

6. These are bubbles in a soda.
   What is it? ___ ___ z z

7. This is a light, drippy rain.
   What is it? ___ ___ ___ z z ___ ___

8. This is the sound a bumblebee makes.
   What is it? ___ ___ z z

**Parent note:** Use with the accompanying sheet.

# Double Z Word Mystery

# Pizza Poetry

**Parent note:** If you've just enjoyed a slice of pizza, this activity is a natural follow-up. Help your child think of different words and phrases that describe pizza. Then help him or her use the directions below to complete each line of the poem.

## Directions:

Line 1: Write one word to describe pizza.

Line 2: Write one flavor word.

Line 3: Write one color word.

Line 4: Write your two favorite pizza toppings.

Line 5: Write one feeling word.

Line 6: Write a different feeling word.

Line 7: Write a different word to describe pizza.

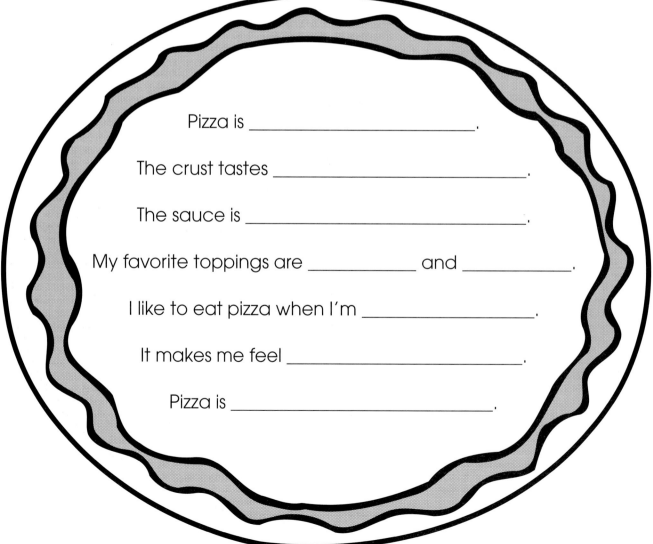

Pizza is _____.

The crust tastes _____.

The sauce is _____.

My favorite toppings are _____ and _____.

I like to eat pizza when I'm _____.

It makes me feel _____.

Pizza is _____.

# Can You Top This?

**Parent note:** There are lots of words that begin with the same letters as those in *pizza pie*, and this partner game is sure to invite some creative thinking. Have your child remove the die from the bag and then cut apart the pizza slices below. Then help your child read and follow the directions to play the pizza writing game. Sounds delicious!

## Directions:

1. Give one slice to your partner.

2. Roll the die.
   Read the letter on top.

3. Find that letter on your slice.
   If the space is blank,
     write a word that begins with that letter.
   If the space already has a word,
     your turn is over.

4. Have your partner repeat Steps 2 and 3, then you repeat Steps 2 and 3, and so on.

5. When one partner has a full slice, the game is over.

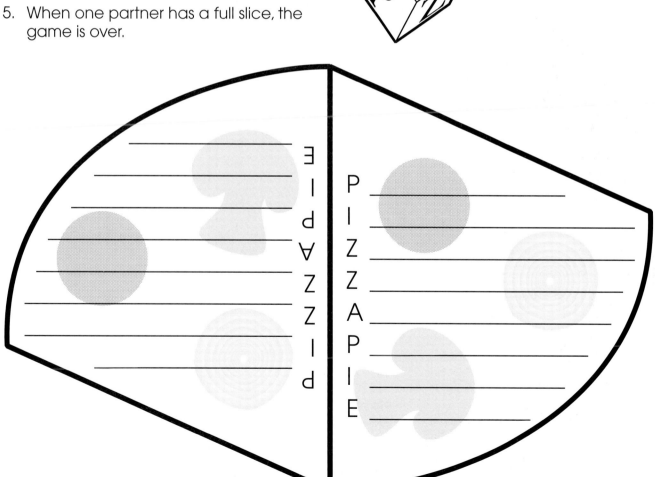

# A Tricky Pizza Puzzle

**Parent note:** If you're planning a pizza meal, this activity makes a great accompaniment. Help your child read and follow the directions below to solve this word puzzle. Then help him or her unscramble the leftover letters to reveal a secret message.

## Directions:

1. There are 12 pizza words hidden in this puzzle. Each word is in the word bank below.

2. Circle each word you find in the puzzle. Cross it off the list.

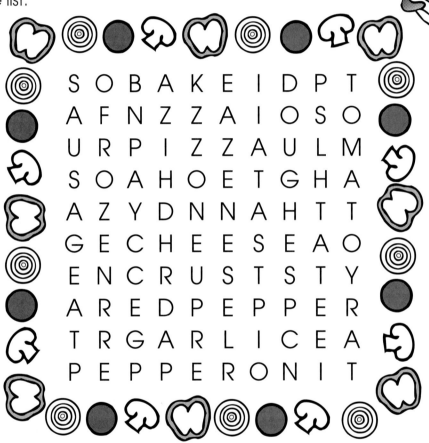

```
S O B A K E I D P T
A F N Z Z A I O S O
U R P I Z Z A U L M
S O A H O E T G H A
A Z Y D N N A H T T
G E C H E E S E A O
E N C R U S T S T Y
A R E D P E P P E R
T R G A R L I C E A
P E P P E R O N I T
```

### Word Bank

| | | | |
|---|---|---|---|
| pizza | crust | sausage | cheese |
| bake | pepperoni | frozen | dough |
| garlic | tomato | red pepper | onions |

### Secret Message

\_\_ \_\_ \_\_ \_\_ \_\_    \_\_ \_\_ \_\_ \_\_ \_\_    \_\_ \_\_ \_\_ \_\_ \_\_ \_\_

\_\_ \_\_ \_\_ \_\_ \_\_    \_\_ \_\_ \_\_ \_\_ \_\_ \_\_    \_\_ \_\_ \_\_ \_\_ \_\_!

# Pumpkin Pickin' Time!

Carve out some special time for learning at home with this bag of pumpkin-themed activities.

## A Plentiful Patch of Books

Scoop up several of these pumpkin books to send home. There's no better way to harvest a good crop of beginning readers!

- *The Biggest Pumpkin Ever* by Steven Kroll
- *Five Little Pumpkins* by Iris Van Rynbach
- *It's Pumpkin Time!* by Zoe Hall
- *Jeb Scarecrow's Pumpkin Patch* by Jana Dillon
- *The Pumpkin Patch* by Elizabeth King
- *Pumpkin Pumpkin* by Jeanne Titherington

## Prized Pumpkin Activities

These blue-ribbon ideas are sure to grow lots of learning opportunities!

| Skill—Activity | Title | Materials |
|---|---|---|
| Creative writing—story | "Where, Oh Where, Did That Pumpkin Go?" | copy of page 124 |
| Observation, recording information—search | "Scavenger Hunt" | copy of page 125, small clipboard |
| Following directions, recognizing differences—search | "Pumpkin Pals" | copy each of pages 126 and 127 |
| Observation—experiment | "Planting Pumpkin Seeds" | copy of page 128, 1 cup of potting soil in a resealable plastic bag, 3 or 4 pumpkin seeds |
| Logical thinking—game | "The Last Seed" | copy of page 129, 15 pumpkin seeds |

PUMPKIN PATCH

## More Pumpkins, Please!

- If you're sending this bag in the fall, include directions to a local pumpkin patch or farmers' market. Enclose a note encouraging parents to take their children to pick out pumpkins just right for carving. (Also let them know of a neighborhood grocery store with a nice pumpkin selection.)
- Challenge parents to work with their youngsters to see how many words they can make from the letters in the word *pumpkins*. Let's see, there's *skip, pun, kin….*
- Send home a note inviting parents to hide a supply of mini pumpkin gourds around the house for little ones to find. Then, as each pumpkin is found, have the child describe its location using positional words, such as *beside, between, above,* and *under.*

# Where, Oh Where, Did That Pumpkin Go?

**Parent note:** Storytelling is a cinch with this activity! Help your child tell the story of a rolling pumpkin by asking questions such as the following: Where did the pumpkin roll? What did the pumpkin do? What happened to the pumpkin? Then help your child read and follow the directions at right to write a creative, fun story in the frame. Encourage your child to read the finished story to family members; then post it in your home for later enjoyment.

### Directions:

1. Look at the picture below.
2. What is happening?

   What will happen next?
3. Write a story about the pumpkin.

   Write in the frame.

# Scavenger Hunt

**Parent note:** Talk with your child about pumpkins—their shape, the color, and the letters in the word. Have your child cut out the pumpkin shape below and then remove the clipboard from the bag. Help your child plan a scavenger hunt around your home, using the categories below. Invite your child to clip the pumpkin cutout to the clipboard and gather a pencil and some crayons. Encourage him or her to set off on the hunt and then illustrate and label each item.

—Find things that are orange.

—Find round things.

—Find things that begin with the letter *P.*

I found…

# Pumpkin Pals

**Parent note:** Talk with your child about carving pumpkins into jack-o'-lanterns. Does your child prefer happy, silly, or scary faces? Have your child remove the accompanying sheet from the bag. Help your child read and follow the directions below to color the pumpkins. For more pumpkin fun, invite your child to draw four jack-o'-lanterns on the back of this page and write a sentence describing each one.

### Directions:

1. Find the pumpkin with triangular eyes.
   Color the eyes and mouth red.

2. Find the smallest pumpkin.
   Color it green.

3. Find the angry pumpkin.
   Color its mouth brown.

4. Find the pumpkin with the longest stem.
   Color the stem green.

5. Find the surprised pumpkin.
   Color it yellow and green.

6. Find the sad pumpkin.
   Color its eyes blue.

7. Find the pumpkin with big eyebrows.
   Color its eyebrows purple.

8. Find the pumpkin with two teeth.
   Color its mouth yellow.

9. Color the uncolored pumpkin shells orange.

©The Education Center, Inc. • *It's in the Bag!* • TEC4100

# Planting Pumpkin Seeds

**Parent note:** What's a pumpkin study without some real pumpkin plants? Help your child read and follow the directions below to grow some pumpkin sprouts. Remind him or her to check the planter every day and draw a picture of what he or she sees. Be sure to water the seeds as needed and open the bag when the sprouts grow tall enough. At the end of the activity, have your child write how the seeds changed. If desired, transplant the sprouts to a large pot and see whether anything interesting happens!

## Directions:

1. Add one-fourth cup of water to the soil.
2. Close the bag and mix.
3. Open the bag.
   Plant the seeds in the soil.
4. Close the bag.
   Put it in a window.
5. Look at your seeds each day.
   Draw what you see.

**PUMPKIN**
SEEDS

| Day 1 | Day 2 | Day 3 |
|-------|-------|-------|
| | | |
| **Day 4** | **Day 5** | **Day 6** |
| | | |
| **Day 7** | **Day 8** | **Day 9** |
| | | |

# The Last Seed

**Parent note:** Here's a simple game to improve your child's logical-thinking and planning skills. Have your child remove the seeds from the bag. Help your child read the directions below. Then play several rounds of the game together. Between rounds, talk with your child about what his or her plan was for the previous round, whether it worked, and what could be done differently next time. Have fun!

## Directions:

1. Put the seeds on the pumpkin.
2. Take turns picking off just one or two seeds.
3. The person who takes the last seed(s) is the winner.

# Revealing Rainbows

Illuminate learning with this bright and beautiful activity bag!

## Rainbow Reading
This colorful collection of literature is just right for your literacy bag.

- *All the Colors of the Rainbow* (Rookie Read-About Science) by Allan Fowler
- *Planting a Rainbow* by Lois Ehlert
- *A Rainbow of My Own* by Don Freeman

## Time to Treasure
What's waiting at the end of this rainbow? Magical moments filled with fun and learning for parents and children.

| Skill—Activity | Title | Materials |
|---|---|---|
| Creative writing—journal | "Colorful Writing" | copy of page 131, three 5" x 7" sheets of blank paper |
| Vocabulary, sounds and letters—word-building activity | "Rainbow Words" | copy of page 132 |
| Following directions, writing to explain—experiment | "Reflected Rainbow" | copy of page 133, aluminum pie pan, small mirror |
| Letter recognition, spelling—game | "Give Me an *R*" | construction paper copy of page 134, paper lunch bag |
| Rhyming, poetry—craft | "Chase Away the Blues" | copy of page 135, different colors of tissue paper, 12" length of yarn, two 7" squares of clear Con-Tact covering (with backing intact and a 6" circle drawn on the front of one square) |
| Color words—game | "Spin and Win" | white construction paper copy of page 136, brad |

## The Rainbow Connection

- If you're sending this bag home during warm months, share with parents this easy way to create a backyard rainbow. Have them stand with their backs to the sun and use a garden hose to spray water in an arch. Ask them to invite their youngsters to run through the rainbows!

- Send a note to parents encouraging them to serve this simple, colorful snack: Make several rainbow colors of gelatin; then scoop a little of each onto a cloud of whipped cream.

- Somewhere over the rainbow…there are lots of sorting opportunities! Encourage parents and youngsters to use Fruity Pebbles cereal, Skittles candy, or jellybeans to sort up a storm.

# Colorful Writing

**Parent note:** Rainbows are fanciful and fun—and sure to trigger your child's imagination! Have your child remove the blank paper from the bag. Then help your child prepare a journal by coloring and cutting out the cover (below) and stapling it to the paper to make a booklet. Talk about the different journal topics with your child and encourage him or her to write and illustrate three of them.

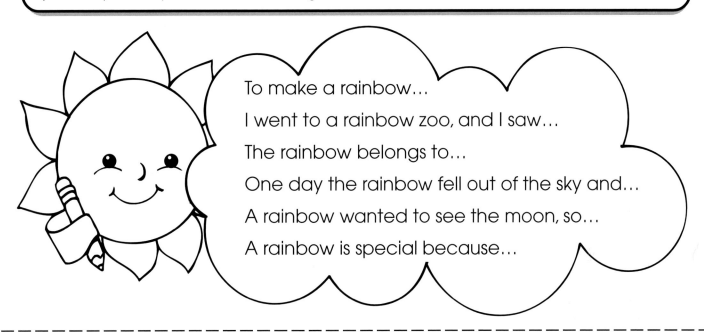

To make a rainbow…

I went to a rainbow zoo, and I saw…

The rainbow belongs to…

One day the rainbow fell out of the sky and…

A rainbow wanted to see the moon, so…

A rainbow is special because…

_____'s Rainbow Journal

**Skills:** *Vocabulary, sounds and letters—word-building activity*

# Rainbow Words

**Parent note:** Try this bright activity for some rainbow fun! Help your child read and follow the directions below, making sure he or she traces each letter with two different crayons to create a rainbow look. When your child reaches Step 3, the word bank below may be a handy reference. Read each new word with your child, and talk about how it relates to rainbows.

**Directions:**

1. Trace each letter two times.

2. Cut out the letters in boxes.

3. Glue to make words.

 ater     ain     ky

pro  ise    l 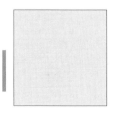 ck

co  ors     eer su

| m | r | s | u |
|---|---|---|---|
| l | ch | w | n |

**Word Bank**

| water | promise |
|-------|---------|
| sky | rain |
| sun | luck |
| cheer | colors |

# Reflected Rainbow

**Parent note:** Reread a nonfiction book about rainbows with your child; then discuss it. Have your child prepare for this simple sunny-day experiment by removing the pie pan and mirror from the bag. He or she will also need a cup of water. Help your child read and follow the directions below to complete the experiment. Here are some success tips: The mirror must be very slightly slanted in order to reflect the sunlight. Put this sheet in front of the mirror and pan; then let the mirror reflect onto the bottom of this sheet. Encourage your child to use the corresponding crayons to color right over the reflection. The result is a rainbow!

## Directions:

1. Put the pan in a sunny spot. Fill it with water.

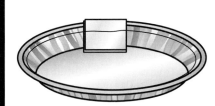

2. Put the mirror in the pan. Write what you think will happen.
   I think _____

   _____

   _____.

3. Put this paper in front of the pan. Tilt the mirror to reflect the sunlight on this paper.

4. Draw what you see.
   Write what happened.

   _____

   _____

# Give Me an *R*

**Parent note:** Invite up to four family members to join in this game. Have your child remove the paper sack from the bag and cut apart the letters below—one set for each player—and put them in the paper sack. Then help your child read and follow the directions below to play the game. What's the best part? Everyone wins!

### Directions:

1. Reach into the sack.

2. Take out seven letters.

3. Try to spell *rainbow*.

4. Take turns trading letters until you can spell *rainbow*.

| R | A | I | N | B | O | W |
|---|---|---|---|---|---|---|
| R | A | I | N | B | O | W |
| R | A | I | N | B | O | W |
| R | A | I | N | B | O | W |

# Chase Away the Blues

**Parent note:** Begin this cheerful keepsake activity by playing a rhyming game with your child. Have him or her say a word; then you say one that rhymes. Switch roles and continue the rhyming fun. Next, have your child remove the Con-Tact covering squares, tissue paper, and yarn from the bag. Help him or her find the square with the circle drawing. Peel off the backing and lay that square sticky side up in front of your child. Help your child read and follow the directions below to complete the craft. When the craft is completed, encourage your child to read the poem to the recipient.

## Directions:

1. Tear bits of tissue paper.

2. Stick them to the circle drawn on the square.

3. Color and cut out the poem.
   Read it.

4. Think of words that rhyme with *blue* and *way.*
   Fill in the blanks.
   Write your name.

5. Stick the poem to the middle of the circle.

6. Find the other square.
   Peel off the backing.
   Stick it over the circle.

7. Cut out the circle.

8. Punch a hole near the top.
   Make a yarn hanger.

9. Give the poem to someone special.
   Read the poem to that person.

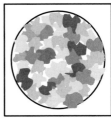

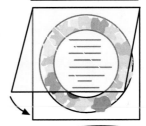

Purple, red, orange, yellow,
green, and blue—
I made this rainbow
just for _____.
Dark clouds may come your way,
But I'll be there to brighten
your _____!

Love,

_____

# Spin and Win

**Parent note:** This game puts a new spin on rainbow color identification! Help your child collect an old magazine for each family member; then read and follow the directions to assemble the spinner. Next, gather the family around and instruct the first player to spin the spinner. Have everyone race to find an object of the designated color in his or her magazine. The first person to show his or her object, point out the color, and spell the color word gets the points indicated on the spinner. Continue in this manner with the second player taking a turn. Play several rounds of the game before tallying scores.

### Directions:

1. Look at the circle.
   Color each part a different color of the rainbow.

2. Cut out the circle and pointer.

3. Make a hole in the circle and pointer.

4. Use a brad to put them together.

5. Spin and win!

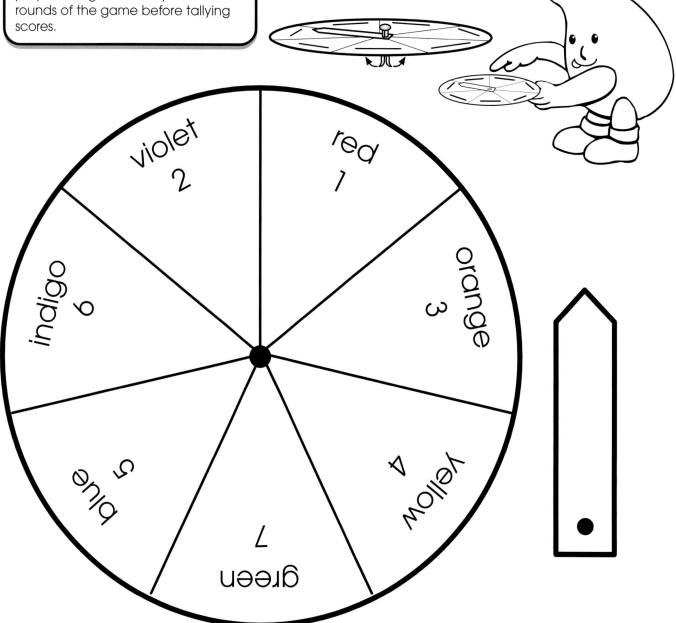

# Let It Snow!

While the weather may be frightful, these activities are just delightful! So let it snow!

### Snow Stories

Snuggle up with a cool book!
- *The First Snowfall* by Anne and Harlow Rockwell
- *Snip, Snip…Snow!* by Nancy Poydar
- *Snow* by Uri Shulevitz
- *Snowballs* by Lois Ehlert
- *The Snowy Day* by Ezra Jack Keats

## Snow, Snow, Snow!

Brrravo! There may be a chill in the air, but these snow-related activities will have youngsters cheering for more.

| Skill—Activity | Title | Materials |
|---|---|---|
| Descriptive writing—booklet | "Snow Walk" | copy of page 138 |
| Reading, number words—game | "Snowflake Scramble" | copy of page 139, 20 game markers in two different colors |
| Compound words—matching activity | "It's Snowing!" | copy of page 140, 9" x 12" sheet of light blue construction paper |
| Reading for information—calendar | "Snow Days!" | copy of page 141 |
| Making words—game | "Chilly Word Fun" | copy of page 142 |
| Following Directions, writing to explain—experiment | "Snowflake Crystals" | copy of page 143 |

### Snowy Surplus

Enclose a note to parents encouraging them to use the recipe below to help their child fingerpaint a wintry scene.

2 c. Ivory Snow powder
1 c. of water

1. Beat with a mixer until stiff.
2. Fingerpaint onto colored construction paper.
3. Let dry.

**Skill:** *Descriptive writing—booklet*

# Snow Walk

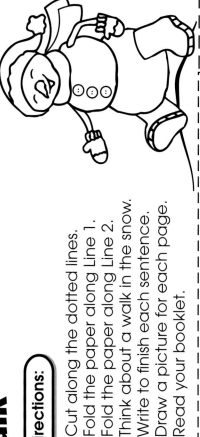

**Parent note:** Discuss with your child things he or she might see, hear, feel, or smell during a walk in the snow. Help your child read and follow the directions to create a folded paper booklet. Now that's some cool reading!

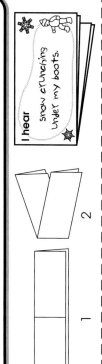

## Directions:

1. Cut along the dotted lines.
2. Fold the paper along Line 1.
3. Fold the paper along Line 2.
4. Think about a walk in the snow.
5. Write to finish each sentence.
6. Draw a picture for each page.
7. Read your booklet.

**Line 1**

### I see

### I hear

©The Education Center, Inc.

### I feel

### I smell

**Line 2**

# Snowflake Scramble

| | |
|---|---|
| Which number is less: 15 or 25? | What number comes after 94? |
| Which number is more: 47 or 26? | What number comes before 6? |
| What is the lowest number on the gameboard? | What even number is between 20 and 24? |
| What even number is between 8 and 12? | What number comes after 99? |
| What odd number is between 8 and 10? | What does 7 + 7 equal? |

**Cards**

**Parent note:** Hurry, scurry—find the flurry! Play this game with your child to help develop his or her number-word recognition skills. Have your child remove the 20 game markers from the bag. Next, assist your child in cutting out the cards on the right, shuffling them, and placing them facedown in a deck. Have your child divide the markers, keeping one color for himself or herself. Help your child read and follow the directions below to play the game.

**Directions:**

1. Choose a card.
   Read aloud the question.
2. Look at the gameboard.
   Try to place a marker on the correct answer before your partner does.
3. Take turns playing until all the cards are gone.
4. Count your markers on the gameboard.
   The player with more markers wins.

## Snowflake Scramble Gameboard

fourteen

five

ten

two

nine

forty-seven

one hundred

ninety-five

fifteen

twenty-two

# It's Snowing!

**Parent note:** There are lots of words that go with snow, and this activity has a blizzard of them! Have your child remove the construction paper from the bag. Then help your child read and follow the directions below to make compound words.

## Directions:

1. Color and cut out the pieces. Lay them on a table.
2. Read each word.
3. Match compound words.
4. Glue each pair onto the construction paper.
5. Write each new word.

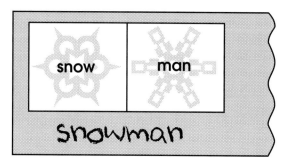

snow | man

Snowman

| | | | |
|---|---|---|---|
| snow | snow | snow | snow |
| snow | snow | snow | snow |
| ball | board | shoe | man |
| plow | bank | storm | flake |

# Snow Days!

**Parent note:** How many snowy days has your child seen this month? Rainy days? Sunny days? After a discussion about the weather in your area, have your child read and interpret this snowy month. Help him or her read the calendar below, color it, and then answer the questions.

## January

| Sunday | Monday | Tuesday | Wednesday | Thursday | Friday | Saturday |
|---|---|---|---|---|---|---|
|  | cloudy 1 | rain 2 | sunny 3 | sunny 4 | cloudy 5 | snow 6 |
| snow 7 | snow 8 | cloudy 9 | cloudy 10 | cloudy 11 | rain 12 | sunny 13 |
| sunny 14 | cloudy 15 | rain 16 | rain 17 | sunny 18 | sunny 19 | snow 20 |
| snow 21 | snow 22 | sunny 23 | cloudy 24 | cloudy 25 | cloudy 26 | snow 27 |
| cloudy 28 | cloudy 29 | cloudy 30 | sunny 31 |  |  |  |

1. How many Saturdays were snowy? _____

2. How many days were sunny? _____

3. Did it rain? _____

4. How many days in all were snowy? _____

5. How many days were cloudy? _____

# Chilly Word Fun

**Parent note:** What's in a word? More words! Help your child cut out the snowflakes below. Assist your child in writing a different letter on each pattern to spell *snowflake*. Next, have your child read and follow the directions to play this partner game.

## Directions:

1. Use the patterns to spell *snowflake*.
2. Take turns moving the letters. Spell a new word each time. Use each letter only once.
3. How many words did you spell?

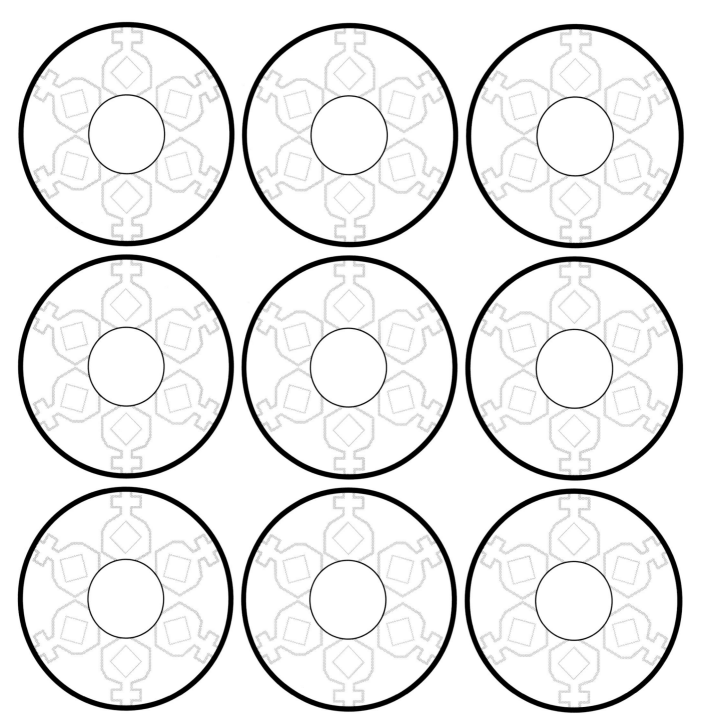

# Snowflake Crystals

**Parent note:** Snowflakes are made of tiny crystals of frozen water. The crystals gather together and then fall to the earth. Making this candy is a tasty way to learn about how other crystals form. Gather the materials for your child; then help him or her tie the string onto the pencil and attach the paper clip as shown. Pour the hot water into the widemouthed jar for your child. Help him or her read and follow the directions below to complete the experiment. Over time, the water will evaporate from the jar and leave the sugar behind. The edible crystals should begin growing in about a week.

**Materials:**
1 c. hot (not boiling) water
2 c. sugar
oven mitt
wooden spoon
food coloring
clean widemouthed jar
pencil
cotton string
clean paper clip

## Directions:

1. Do not touch the hot water.
2. Add a few drops of food coloring to it.
   Stir with the wooden spoon.
3. Add the sugar.
   Stir until the sugar is all gone.
4. Let it cool.
5. Lay the pencil on top of the jar.
   Let the string and paper clip hang in the water.
6. Put the jar in a quiet place.
7. Look for crystals each day for two weeks.
8. On the back of this sheet, draw a picture of the crystals. Taste them.
   Write about how they taste.

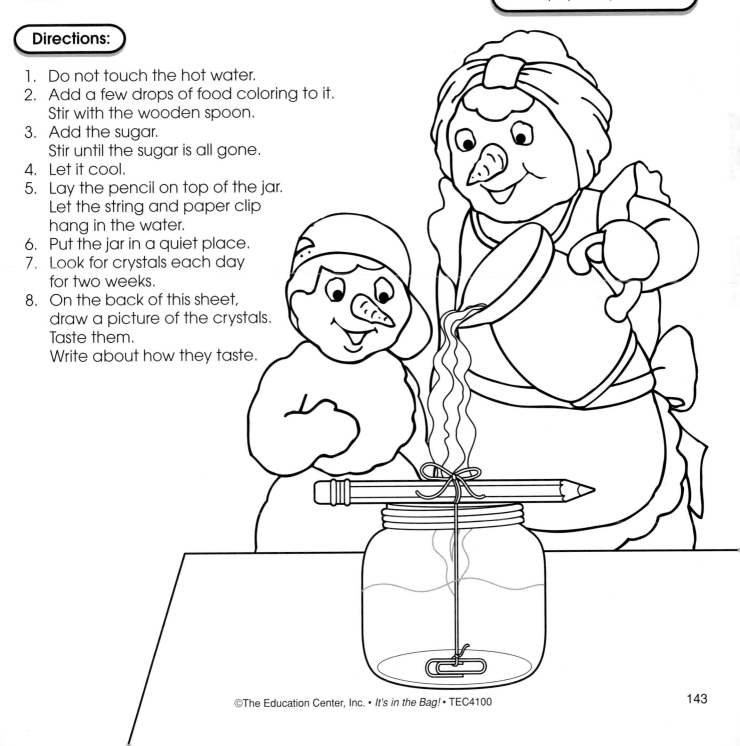

# Out in Space

Count down to literacy exploration with this exciting space unit!

## Books That Twinkle

Choose from this selection of books to shuttle youngsters into the perfect atmosphere for reading!
- *Big Silver Space Shuttle* by Ken Wilson-Max
- *I Wonder Why Stars Twinkle and Other Questions About Space* by Carole Stott
- *Martian Rock* by Carole Diggory Shields
- *Me and My Place in Space* by Joan Sweeney
- *Zoom! Zoom! Zoom! I'm Off to the Moon* by Dan Yaccarino

## Space Gear

Prepare for liftoff by placing a variety of these activities in the bag. Boots—check. Helmet—check. Literacy—check plus!

| Skill—Activity | Title | Materials |
|---|---|---|
| Descriptive writing—booklet | "Blast Off Into Writing!" | copy of page 145, five $4^1/_4$" x $5^1/_2$" sheets of blank paper stapled into a booklet |
| Reading, oral language—game | "Reach for the Stars!" | copy of *I Wonder Why Stars Twinkle and Other Questions About Space* by Carole Stott, white construction paper copies of pages 146 and 147 |
| Creative writing—story starter, craft | "I'm an Astronaut!" | copy of page 148, sheet of 12" x 18" construction paper, sheet of finger-paint paper, 2 small plastic jars of fingerpaint in different colors |
| Oral language, movement—song | "Space Song" | copy of the top of page 149 |
| Vocabulary—cooking | "Frozen Rockets" | copy of the bottom of page 149 |

## Splashdown!

- For more space fun, enclose a note encouraging each family to engage in some space-related dramatic play. Include the following quick costume tips: moon boots made by tying a giant cellulose sponge onto each foot and a kid-sized spacesuit made by cutting a face opening and armholes in a paper grocery bag as shown. Hello, NASA? We're ready!

- Send home a photocopy of a constellation map with a note encouraging families to have a "moon picnic" outside one night and search for stars.

# Blast Off Into Writing!

**Parent note:** Here's a fun writing activity to use after reading about space rockets and space shuttles. Talk with your child about how these crafts blast into space, what they do in space, and how they return to Earth. Next, have your child color and cut out the pictures below. Encourage your child to study each picture and then put them all in the order of a space mission. Invite him or her to describe what's happening in each picture. Then have your child remove the blank booklet from the bag. Help your child read and follow the directions to complete the booklet. 3…2…1…Blast off!

## Directions:

1. Draw a space picture on the cover.
   Write a title.
   Write your name.

2. Look at the first page of the booklet.
   Glue on the first picture.

3. Write a sentence about the picture.

4. Repeat Steps 2 and 3 for the rest of the pages.

5. Color the pictures.

6. Read your space booklet.

# Reach for the Stars!

## Directions:

1. Put the cards in a pile on the gameboard.

2. In turn, answer the true/false questions.

3. For each correct answer, put that card on the rocket path.
   If the answer is incorrect, put the card under the pile.

4. The first player to reach the star wins!

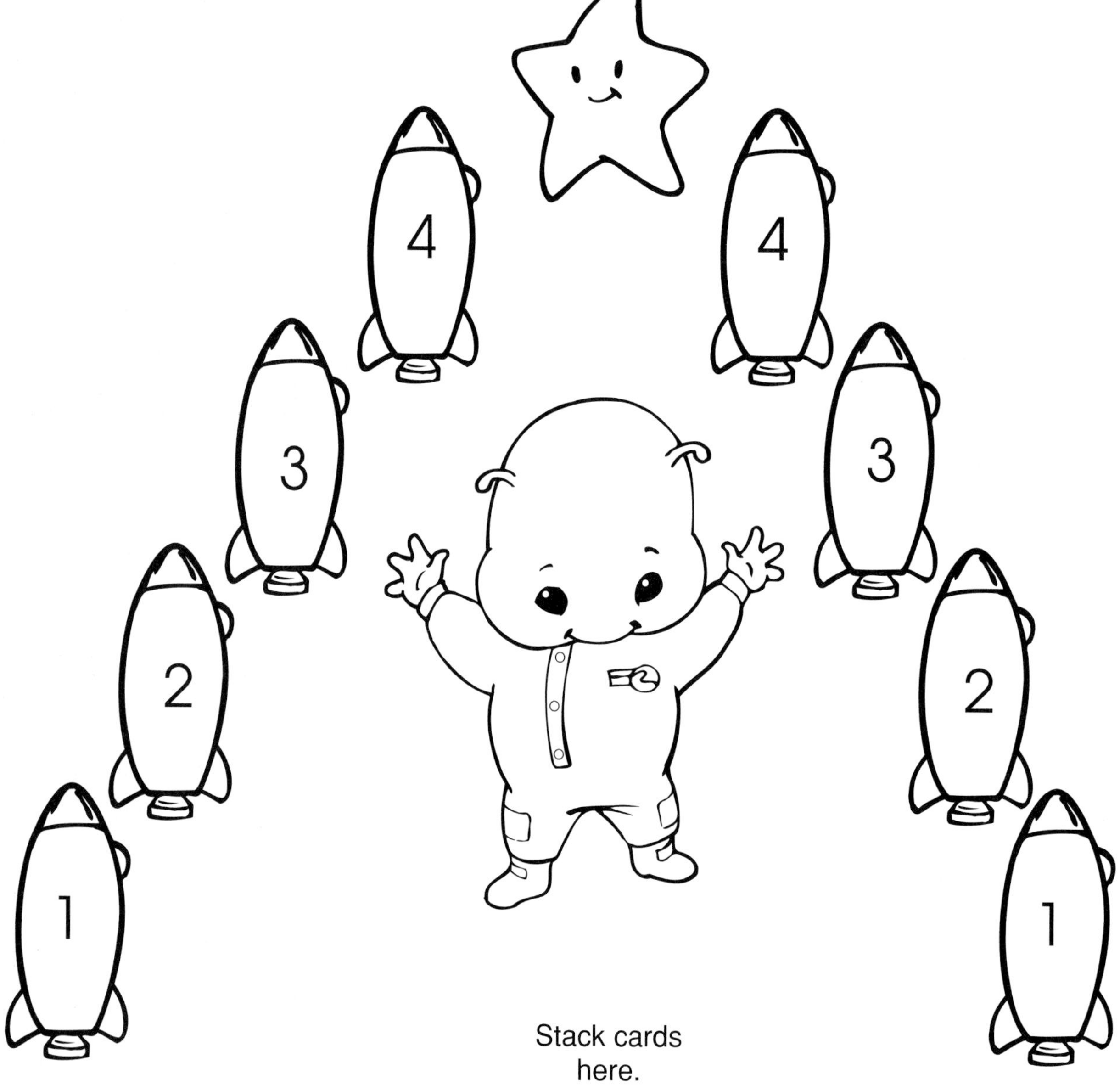

Stack cards here.

Player 1's rocket path

Player 2's rocket path

| | | | |
|---|---|---|---|
| The sun is really a star. | True | The earth is not a planet. | False; It is the third planet from the sun. |
| There are 12 planets. | False; There are nine planets. | People have never walked on the moon. | False; Neil Armstrong was the first man to walk on the moon. |
| The center of the solar system is the moon. | False; The sun is the center of the solar system. | A person who visits space is called a flyer. | False; A person who visits space is called an astronaut. |
| Pluto is the name of a planet. | True | Some planets have rings. | True |
| The Milky Way is made of chocolate. | False; It is made of billions of stars. | Stars are star-shaped. | False; Stars are shaped like balls. |
| Some planets are surrounded by gases. | True | Neptune is called the Red Planet. | False; Mars is called the Red Planet. |

# I'm an Astronaut!

**Parent note:** Who doesn't want to be an astronaut when they grow up? Talk with your child about what it would be like to be an astronaut, and encourage him or her to imagine discovering a new planet. Next, cover a work area with newspaper and dress your child in an old shirt. Have your child remove the construction paper, slick paper, and jars of fingerpaint from the bag and put them on the workspace. Invite him or her to fingerpaint on the slick paper. When the paint is dry, help your child cut out an imaginary planet and then glue it to the construction paper. Then help your child use the story starter below to write a creative story in the space provided. Have your child cut out the story and glue it to the construction paper. Encourage your child to display the finished piece in your home.

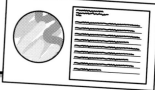

I am an astronaut out in space.
I have just found a brand-new place!
It is...

_____

_____

_____

_____

_____

_____

_____

# Space Song

Round, round, round the sun
The planets like to go.
Floating high in the sky,
A solar system show!

Up, up a rocket blasts,
Off to see the show.
Flying high in the sky,
Above the earth below!

©The Education Center, Inc. • *It's in the Bag!* • TEC4100

---

# Frozen Rockets

**Ingredients for two:**
banana
Magic Shell ice-cream
   topping
toppings such as
   sprinkles, chopped
   nuts, or coconut

**Utensils and supplies:**
plastic knife
2 Popsicle sticks
plastic wrap
spoon
bowl
plate
2 miniature muffin liners
napkins

### Directions for two:

1. **Peel** the banana.
   Cut it in half to make two rockets.
2. Put a **stick** in the end of each rocket.
3. Wrap the rockets in plastic wrap.
4. Freeze the **rockets** for two hours.
   While you are waiting, put the dry
   toppings on the plate.

5. Hold a frozen rocket over the **bowl**.
   Pour Magic Shell over it.
   Spoon up the drips and use them too.
6. **Roll** the rocket in the toppings.
7. Put a muffin-liner bottom on your rocket.
8. Blast off!

©The Education Center, Inc. • *It's in the Bag!* • TEC4100

# Spectacular Spiders

Capture lots of interest with this unit featuring nature's most fascinating eight-legged wonders.

### Weave a Web of Spider Stories

Invite youngsters to examine spiders more closely with this web of fact and fiction.

- *Anansi the Spider: A Tale From the Ashanti* by Gerald McDermott
- *Dream Weaver* by Jonathan London
- *Miss Spider's Tea Party* by David Kirk
- *Spectacular Spiders* by Linda Glaser
- *Spiders* by Gail Gibbons
- *The Very Busy Spider* by Eric Carle

### Super Spider Fun!

Send your little ones skedaddling home with a selection of these stupendous spider ideas!

| Skill—Activity | Title | Materials |
|---|---|---|
| Creative writing—journal | "Spin a Spider Story" | copy of page 151, two 9" x 9" black construction paper squares, five 9" x 9" blank paper squares, plastic container (with a tight-fitting lid) with white washable tempera paint and a marble inside |
| Positional words—craft, booklet | "Spider's Journey" | copy each of pages 152 and 153, large paper clip, $1/2$" pom-pom, 1" pom-pom, 2 chenille stems cut in half, one 18" length of yarn, sheet of waxed paper |
| Descriptive words—poem | "A Spider Poem" | copy of page 154, 12" length of yarn |
| Vocabulary, science—cooking | "Spider Snack" | copy of page 155 |

### Spider Specials

- Include a note suggesting that family members take a walk around their neighborhood to look for and observe real spiders. For times of the year when spiders may not be as visible, suggest that each family go to the library to do research on these eight-legged creatures.

- Tuck a ball of yarn into the bag with a note suggesting that the family work together to weave a web. Have family members stand in a circle. One person holds the end of the yarn and tosses (or rolls) the ball to another person. That person holds the yarn and tosses the ball to someone else. The family continues holding and tossing the yarn until there is a wonderful web. The tricky part is unweaving it! The person holding the ball must send it back to the person who gave it to him. This continues until all the yarn is rerolled into the ball. Happy weaving!

# Spin a Spider Story

### Directions:

1. Cut out a story starter.
2. Glue it to a page.
3. Write a story.
4. Read your story.

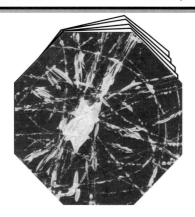

Three happy spiders came into my room. I...

One day I came home to find a spider in...

My pet spider likes to...

I saw a spider acting silly. He was...

One day my spider told me a secret. She said...

# Spider's Journey

**Parent note:** Just like spiders in nature, this nifty activity includes a spider on the move! Have your child remove from the bag the paper clip, pom-poms, chenille stems, waxed paper, length of yarn, and the accompanying sheet. To make a spider, have your child wrap each chenille stem around the paper clip as shown. Then ask your child to put the paper clip on the waxed paper and squeeze a generous amount of glue on it. Next, have your youngster place the pom-poms on the paper clip to complete the spider. Allow it to dry overnight. Then have your child color, cut out, and staple together the cover and booklet pages. After your child personalizes the cover, help him or her hole-punch the upper left corner of the booklet and attach the spider with the yarn. Help your child read and act out the booklet.

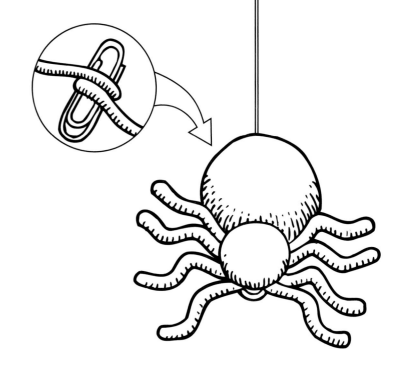

Then the spider dropped **down** on me! 4

Spider's Journey

by

_____

The spider jumped **over** a rock.

1

The spider ran **under** a bush.

2

The spider climbed **up** a big tree.

3

Then the spider dropped **down** on me!

4

# A Spider Poem

**Parent note:** Hairy scary arachnids! Help your child brainstorm descriptive words and phrases about spiders. Then help your child read and follow the directions below to complete this descriptive spider poem.

**Directions:**

1. Think of words that describe spiders.
2. Write one word on each leg.
3. Read your spider poem to your family.
4. Cut out the spider poem.
5. Punch a hole near the top.
   Tie on a yarn hanger.
6. Hang your spider poem.

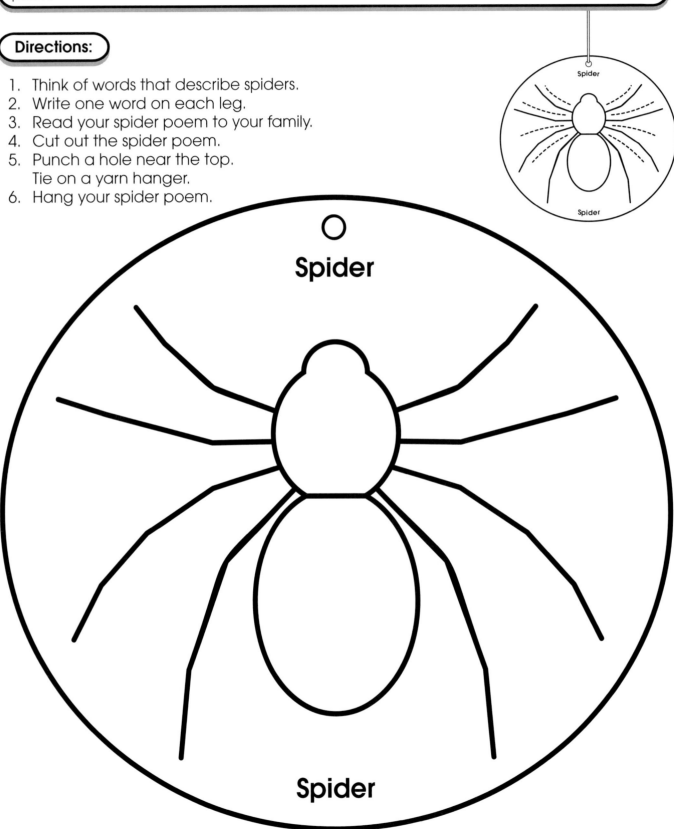

154    

# Spider Snack

**Parent note:** These sweet cookie spiders are just the thing to help your child understand how a real spider's body looks! Help your child read and follow the recipe below, paying special attention to the boldfaced vocabulary words. Before eating, have your child label the diagram below to compare the spider snack to a picture of the real thing.

**Ingredients:**
2 chocolate sandwich cookies (body parts)
chocolate frosting
eight 3" pieces of licorice lace (legs)
8 mini chocolate chips (eyes)

**Utensils and supplies:**
paper plate
plastic knife

**Directions:**

1.  Add eight **legs** to one body part.
2.  Place the body parts next to each other.
3.  Put frosting on the top of your **spider.**
4.  Add eight **eyes** to the body part with legs.
5.  Look at the picture of a real spider.
    Compare.
    Label your snack spider.
6.  **Eat** your snack!

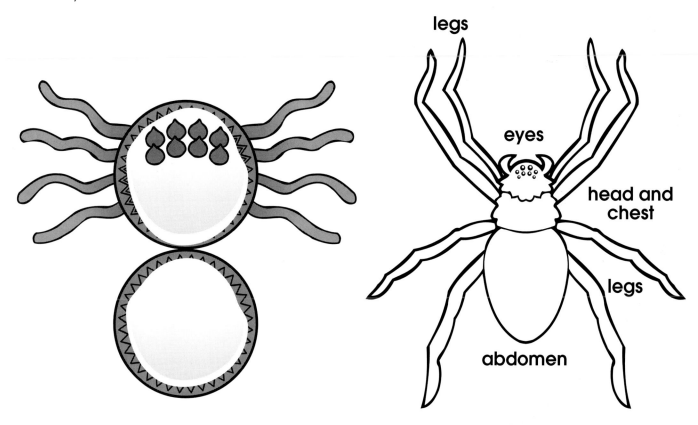

legs

eyes

head and chest

legs

abdomen

# Terrific Teeth

These toothy take-home activities are sure to put a smile on everyone's face!

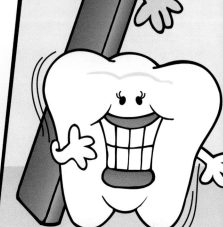

### Teeth Tales

Include the following titles in your bag to encourage little ones to brush up on their reading and listening skills!

- *Doctor De Soto* by William Steig
- *I Know Why I Brush My Teeth* by Kate Rowan
- *Little Rabbit's Loose Tooth* by Lucy Bate
- *My Dentist, My Friend* by P. K. Hallinan

### Bite Into the Curriculum

Sink your teeth into these ideas celebrating good dental health.

| Skill—Activity | Title | Materials |
|---|---|---|
| Writing questions—tooth fairy note | "Just Wondering…" | copy of page 157 |
| Recording information, following directions—chart | "Brush, Brush, Brush!" | white construction paper copy of page 158 |
| Story problems—math activity | "Cashing In" | copy of page 159, assortment of realistic plastic coins (at least 20 pennies, 10 dimes, 7 nickels) *Can reprogram the money amounts according to individual abilities |
| Spelling—puzzle | "Keep Out the Cavities" | copy of page 160 |
| Recalling details, oral language—puzzle | "Say Cheese!" | copy of page 161 |

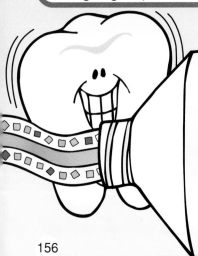

### Keep Chewin'!

- Just how many baby teeth are left? Send home a note suggesting that parents have their child look into a mirror to count baby teeth and then brush them.
- Encourage parents to take their family to a neighborhood dentist for a tour. Enclose a blank notecard and envelope and invite the child to write the dentist a thank-you note.
- Send home a note encouraging parents to help their children make collages from magazine pictures of tooth-friendly foods.

# Just Wondering...

**Parent note:** Talk to your child about the magical tooth fairy. Have your youngster imagine where the tooth fairy lives, what she looks like, and what her favorite color is. Then direct your child to cut out the tooth pattern below. Help him or her write a question or two to the tooth fairy. If desired, continue the activity by having your child put the note under his or her pillow. After your child falls asleep, remove the note and replace it with a response from the tooth fairy. For a magical touch, glue a little glitter (fairy dust) around the edges of the note. When your child wakes up, encourage him or her to look for the response and then read it aloud.

## Directions:

1. Cut out the tooth.
2. Write a question or two.
3. Write your name.
4. Put the note under your pillow.
5. Go to sleep.
   In the morning, look for an answer!

Dear Tooth Fairy,

I was just wondering... _____

_____

_____

_____

_____

_____

Love,

_____

©The Education Center, Inc.

# Brush, Brush, Brush!

**Parent note:** Help your child read and follow the directions to make the toothbrush. Encourage your child to use the toothbrush to practice proper brushing techniques (pretending to have the brush inside his or her mouth). Then help your child fill in the brushing times on the chart and check the corresponding box after each real brushing. When your child has brushed for two weeks, draw a big, toothy grin in the large box (or stick on a smiley-face sticker). What a VIB (Very Important Brusher)!

## Directions:

1. Color the toothbrush.
2. Cut on the bold lines.
3. Fold the sides in along the dotted line.
4. Draw bristles.

Fold here.

Fold here.

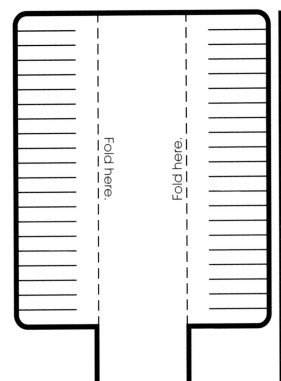

## Toothbrushing Tips

Brush in little circles.

Brush the fronts and then the backs of all your teeth.

## Hooray for Me!

### I Brushed!

| | Sun. | Mon. | Tues. | Wed. | Thurs. | Fri. | Sat. |
|---|---|---|---|---|---|---|---|
| week 1 | | | | | | | |
| week 2 | | | | | | | |

**My Terrific Teeth!**
I will brush at these times each day:

_____
_____

# Cashing In

**Parent note:** Help your child read each of the story problems below. Then help him or her use the coins provided to figure out how much money the tooth fairy will give.

**Directions:**

1. Read.
2. Use money to find the answers.
3. Write the answers.

You lose 20 teeth. The tooth fairy gives you 1¢ for each tooth. How much money does she give you in all?

_____

You lose 10 teeth. The tooth fairy gives you 10¢ for each tooth. How much money does she give you in all?

_____

You lose 5 teeth. The tooth fairy gives you 10¢ for each tooth. How much money does she give you in all?

_____

You lose 7 teeth. The tooth fairy gives you 5¢ for each tooth. How much money does she give you in all?

_____

You lose 14 teeth. The tooth fairy gives you 1¢ for each tooth. How much money does she give you in all?

_____

# Keep Out the Cavities

**Parent note:** Help your child crack the secret code to unveil this hidden message. Simply have your child write the uppercase alphabet in order on a sheet of paper and then number each letter. Then have him or her fill in each blank with the letter that corresponds to the numbered alphabet sequence. To read the message, have your child hold the tooth in front of a mirror and look at its image. Then invite your child to hang the tooth near the bathroom mirror for a daily reminder to brush away the icky sticky!

## Directions:

1. Fill in the missing letters.
2. Hold the tooth in front of a mirror.
3. Read.

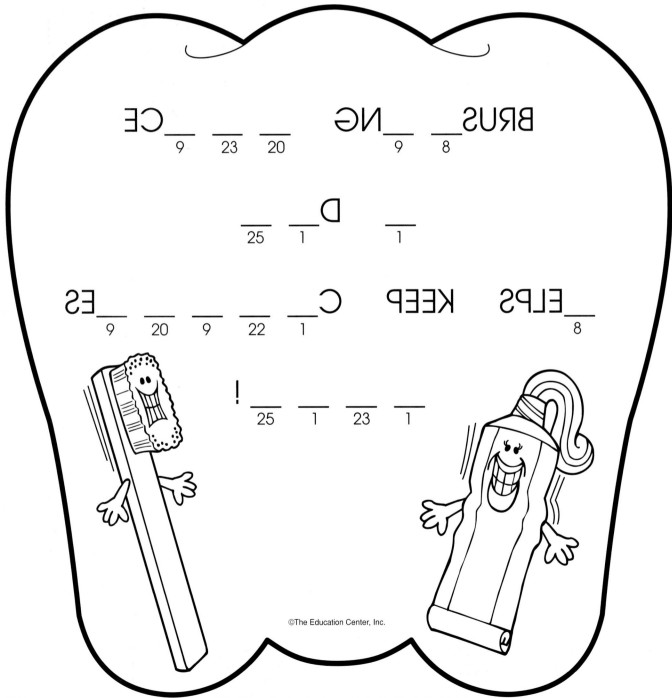

# Say Cheese!

**Parent note:** Review with your child the different ways to keep teeth healthy, such as brushing, flossing, visiting a dentist regularly, and avoiding too many sweets. Then help your child read the directions below to complete the puzzle. Encourage your child to explain the choices as he or she works.

## Directions:

1. Look at the pictures.
   Read the words.

2. Talk about which ones are healthy for teeth.

3. Color only those pictures.
   Make a path from one smile to the other.

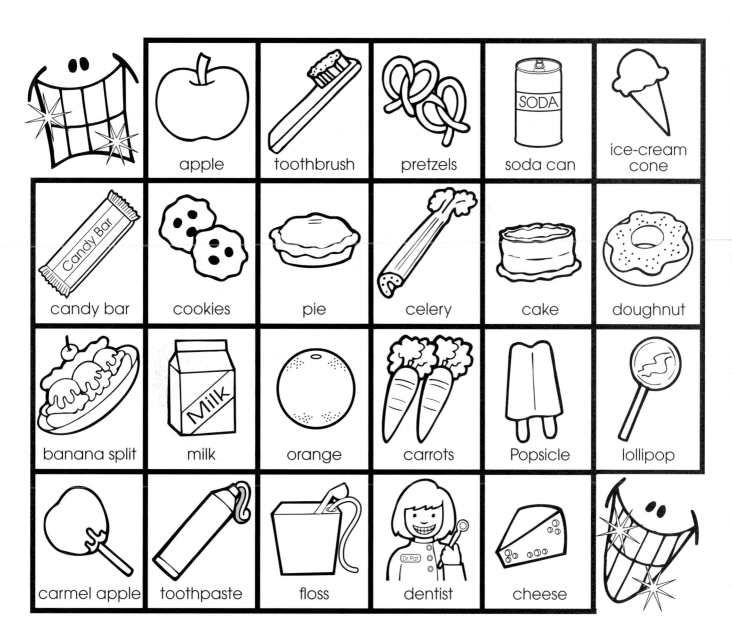

# Going My Way?

Whether it's by land, sea, or sky, these ideas will take your little ones on a journey filled with learning!

## Along for the Ride
Set things in motion with this collection of transportation literature.

- *The Adventures of Taxi Dog* by Debra and Sal Barracca
- *Bicycle Book* by Gail Gibbons
- *The Big Book of Things That Go* by Caroline Bingham
- *School Bus* by Donald Crews
- *Sheep in a Jeep* by Nancy Shaw

## Pack Your Bag!
Rev up your youngsters' engines with a selection of ideas that will really help learning take off!

| Skill—Activity | Title | Materials |
|---|---|---|
| Classifying, oral language—chart | "Getting Around" | copy of page 163, old magazine, sheet of blank paper |
| Creative writing—craft | "Cleared for Takeoff" | white construction paper copy of page 164, paper clip |
| Reading—incentive | "Reading Railroad" | white construction paper copy of page 165 |
| Writing words—list, trip plan | "My Trip" | copy of page 166 |
| Sequencing—story cards | "Off to School" | copy of page 167, sentence strip |
| Vocabulary—cooking | "The Peanut Butter Express" | copy of the top of page 168 |
| Oral language—song | "Off They Go!" | copy of the bottom of page 168 |

## An Added Excursion
- For more transportation fun, include a note encouraging each child to design a new mode of transportation. Suggest that the child use milk cartons, soda bottles, or paper towel tubes to construct the new form of transportation.

- Send home a note suggesting a family field trip to observe different modes of transportation. Places to consider include the airport to watch planes take off and land or a marina to watch boats sail in and out of port.

Skills: *Classifying, oral language—chart*

# Getting Around

**Parent note:** What's the best way to get from point A to point B? It depends on how you want to get there! This sorting activity is just right for encouraging your child to think creatively about transportation. Have your child remove the magazine from the bag. Look through it together, and assist your child in cutting out pictures of different forms of transportation, such as cars, boats, bicycles, trains, or planes. Encourage your child to name each picture and then place it into the appropriate column below. Invite him or her to explain why each picture belongs in that category and then glue it in place. (If more space is needed, glue the blank sheet of paper to the bottom of the page.) Talk about the chart results together.

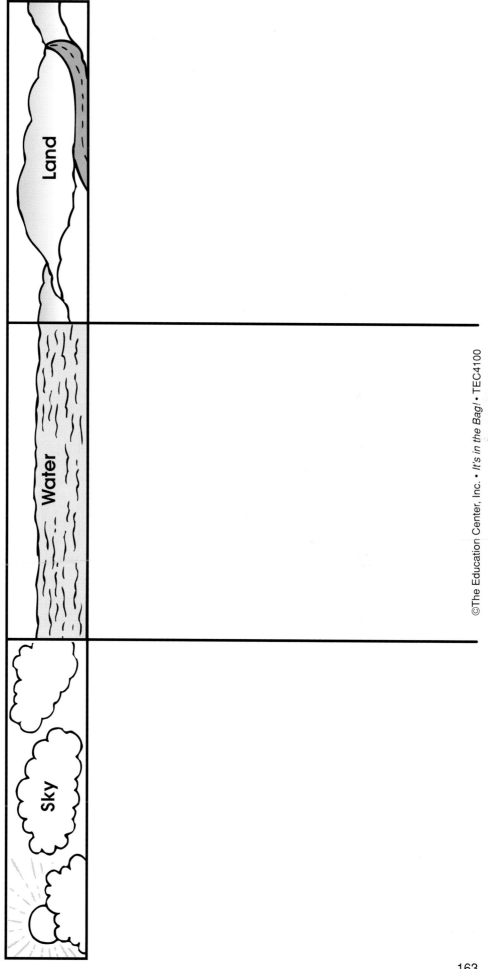

# Cleared for Takeoff

**Parent note:** Expect a smooth flight with this creative-writing activity! Have your child remove the paper clip from the bag. Next, help your child read and follow the directions to make a paper plane. Invite your child to fly it several times, each time moving the paper clip to a different spot on the plane. Ask your child if some paper clip spots helped the plane fly better than others. Then have your youngster remove the paper clip, unfold the plane, and write a story on it about an imaginary, adventurous airplane ride.

## Directions:

1. Color the plane.

2. Cut it out.

3. Fold the plane on the dotted lines.

4. Put a paper clip on the front of the plane.

5. Fly your plane.

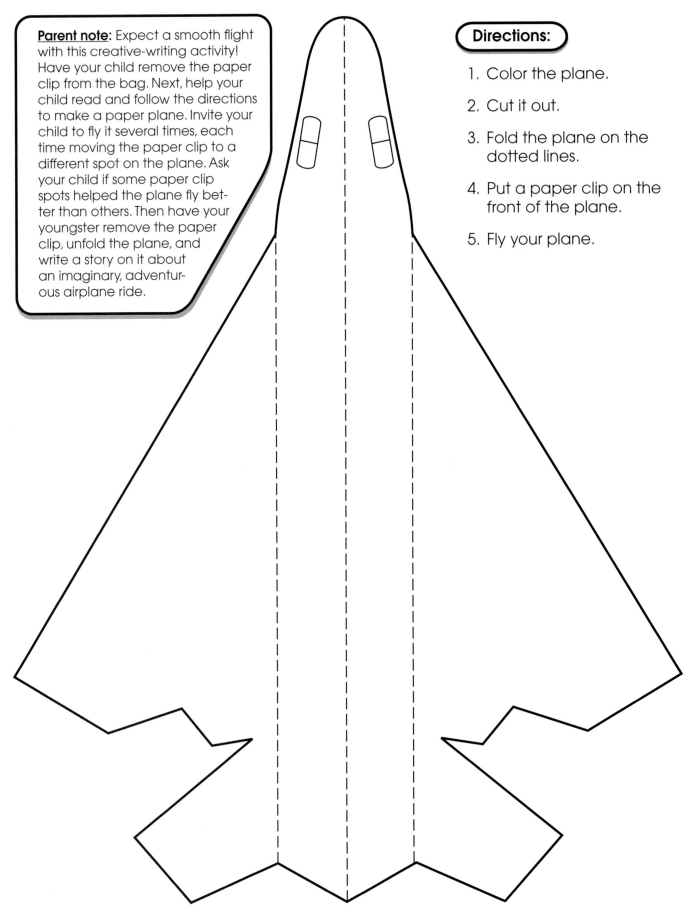

# Reading Railroad

**Parent note:** Toot, toot—all aboard the reading train! Encourage your child to read with this imaginative train. Display the train engine in a prominent place. Each time your child reads a book, present him or her with a train car. Help your child record the title and author on the car and then tape it to the end of the train. Trace the last car to make several copies and inspire even more reading practice.

Clickety-clack!
Clickety-clack!
The reading train
is right on track!

_____
Title:

Author:

_____
Title:

Author:

_____
Title:

Author:

_____
Title:

Author:

_____
Title:

Author:

_____
Title:

Author:

_____
Title:

Author:

_____
Title:

Author:

_____
Title:

Author:

_____
Title:

Author:

# My Trip

I am going on a trip today.

I will take a _____ to _____. Hooray!
<small>(transportation)</small>     <small>(place)</small>

I will pack _____

_____

_____ .

©The Education Center, Inc. • *It's in the Bag!* • TEC4100

# Off to School

**Parent note:** So what's it like to ride the school bus? Talk about a bus ride with your child. If your child doesn't ride the school bus, help him or her remember a city bus ride, a carpool, or a similar event when a friend was picked up. Next, have your child remove the sentence strip from the bag. Instruct your child to cut the story cards apart. Help your child read the sentence on each card, put the cards in order, and then glue them to the strip. Encourage your child to retell the story, and then continue by telling about the bus ride home after school.

We arrive at school.

"See you after school!"

We get off the bus.

"Good morning!" We get on the bus.

We pick up Sam.

We ride the bus to the next stop.

# The Peanut Butter Express

**Parent note:** This tasty train car is just the ticket for healthy snacking! Help your child gather enough ingredients and supplies to make a train car for each family member. Next, paying special attention to the boldfaced vocabulary words, help your child read and follow the directions below. When the snacks are ready, encourage your child to line them up to make a train; then invite each family member to enjoy a train car. Chew! Chew!

**Ingredients:**
1 graham cracker sheet
   (train car)
peanut butter
2 banana slices
pretzel sticks

**Utensils and supplies:**
paper plate
plastic knife

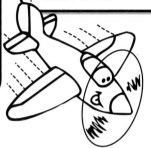

**Directions:**

1. Spread peanut butter on a graham cracker **train** car.
2. Add two banana slice **wheels.**
3. Add pretzels to make **windows** and a **door.**
4. Repeat Steps 1–3 for each train **car.**

©The Education Center, Inc. • *It's in the Bag!* • TEC4100

---

# Off They Go!

**Parent note:** The wild blue yonder is calling! Help your child read and sing the song below. Ask your child to think of movements to accompany each verse. Then help your child create new verses, each including a different mode of transportation.

*(sung to the tune of "Down by the Station")*

Down by the airport,
Early in the morning.
See the little airplanes
All in a row.
See the ground controller
Wave a little flag.
Woosh, woosh, woosh, woosh!
Off they go!

Down by the boatyard,
Early in the morning.
See the little sailboats
All in a row.
See the busy sailors
Raise the giant sails.
Splish, splash, splish, splash!
Off they go!

Down by the schoolyard,
Early in the morning.
See the little buses
All in a row.
See the bus drivers
Start up their engines.
Beep, beep, vroom, vroom!
Off they go!

©The Education Center, Inc. • *It's in the Bag!* • TEC4100

# Turkey Time

Gobble, gobble…a turkey is a funny bird
that wobbles, wobbles, wobbles!

## Turkey Tales
Enjoy this spread of turkey tales!

- *All About Turkeys* by Jim Arnosky
- *Gracias, the Thanksgiving Turkey* by Joy Cowley
- *A Turkey for Thanksgiving* by Eve Bunting
- *'Twas the Night Before Thanksgiving* by Dav Pilkey
- *Wild Turkeys* by Dorothy Hinshaw Patent

## Gobble, Gobble!
Youngsters and their families will strut right through these turkey-themed activities!

| Skill—Activity | Title | Materials |
| --- | --- | --- |
| Writing lists, creative writing—story | "Turkey Time" | copy of page 170 |
| Comprehension—story | "Fruitful Harvest" | copy of page 171 |
| Descriptive words—craft | "Turkey Treat Favors" | white construction paper copy of page 172, 5½ oz. Styrofoam coffee cup, 9" x 12" sheet each of orange and red construction paper |
| Vocabulary—cooking | "Gobbling Gobblers" | copy of page 173 |
| Beginning consonants—game | "*T* Is for Turkey" | copy of page 174 |

## Trottin' Along
- For feathers-on fun, include in the bag several sheets of white construction paper, a watercolor paint set, and several craft feathers to use as paint-brushes. Also tuck in a note encouraging parents to help their child paint pictures and then write a sentence about each.
- Enclose a note encouraging families to count all the frozen turkeys the next time they visit the grocery store.

# Turkey Time

**Parent note:** A good way to begin a turkey story is with a list of words about turkeys. Talk with your child about turkeys; ask what they eat, how they live, how they look, what they do. Next, help your child create a list of five turkey-related words, writing one on each feather. Then help him or her use each word to write a creative story about turkeys on the back of this sheet.

# Fruitful Harvest

**Parent note:** Gobble, gobble—it's time for Mr. Turkey's annual harvest party! Help your child read the story below and answer the questions. Encourage your child to complete the story, give it a title, and then illustrate it on the back of this sheet. Now that sounds like a terrific party!

Mr. Turkey bought 5 pears for his harvest party. They looked so tasty that Mr. Turkey had to try one. He ate all the pears, so he bought 4 more. He also bought 3 red apples and some nuts. He bought vegetables for soup and 3 pumpkins.

Mr. Turkey went home and made a big pot of soup. He made applesauce. He made 4 pumpkin pies topped with nuts. He ate the pears.

Then Mr. Turkey waited for his friends to arrive. The doorbell rang and then…

How many pears did Mr. Turkey buy all together? _____

How many apples did he buy? _____

When Mr. Turkey got home, what did he do? _____

How many pumpkin pies did he make? _____

What happened to the pears? _____

What happened when the doorbell rang? Complete the story. Write on the back of this sheet if you need more space.

_____

_____

_____

_____

_____

_____

_____

# Turkey Treat Favors

**Parent note:** Well, "wattle" you know? Somebody's going to be thankful for this treat! First, have your child remove the cup and construction paper from the bag. Cut a slit in the cup as shown; then help your child cut out the feather pattern and trace it three times on each sheet of construction paper. Next, encourage your child to think of a special person who would like to have this treat. Have him or her write that person's name on the cup. Help your child read and follow the directions to complete the turkey treat favor.

### Directions:

1. Look at a feather.
   Write one word that tells about your special person.
2. Repeat for each feather.
3. Put the bottom of each feather into the slit on the cup.
   Glue each feather onto the back of the cup.
4. Cut out the head pattern.
   Color it red.
5. Cut a slit on the dotted line.
   Slide it over the front of the cup.
6. Fill the cup with a snack, such as popcorn.
7. Give the treat to your special person.

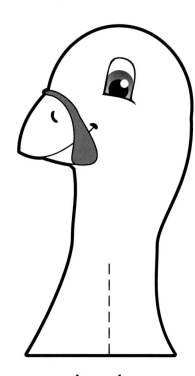

**head**

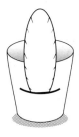 

**feather**

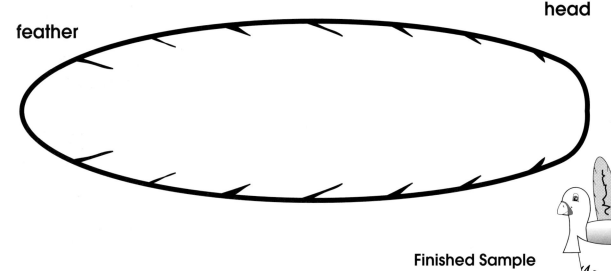

**Finished Sample**

# Gobbling Gobblers

**Parent note:** Mmmm—do you smell turkey? It's not the real thing, but this sweet cookie turkey is a fun dessert your child can easily make. Gather the ingredients and utensils with your child. Then, paying special attention to the boldfaced vocabulary words, help your child read and follow the recipe below to make a gobbler.

**Ingredients:**
sandwich cookie
cinnamon Imperial Candy (head)
malted milk ball (body)
7 pieces of candy corn (feathers)
1 tbsp. of frosting

**Utensils and supplies:**
tablespoon
napkins

### Directions:

1. Twist apart the **cookie.**
   Leave all the cream filling on one side.

2. Dip the red candy **head** in the frosting.
   Stick it on the malted milk ball **body.**

3. Dip the body in the frosting.
   Stick it in the center of the cookie with the cream.

4. Spread frosting on the plain cookie half.
   Stick on the candy corn feathers.
   Stand it behind the other cookie.

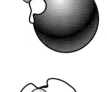

# *T* Is for Turkey

**Parent note:** *Turkeys, trains, tacos…what on earth could these things have in common? Exactly—they all begin with* t! *Discuss beginning letters with your child and have him or her point out a few in a book or magazine. Then help your child read and cut out the game cards below. Help him or her divide the cards (facedown) into two equal stacks, one for each player. Then play this variation of the traditional card game Slapjack. Players take turns turning over one card and placing it in a center pile. When a card with a word beginning with the letter* t *comes up, each player tries to slap the pile first to get all the cards. Play continues until one player is out of cards.*

| | | | |
|---|---|---|---|
| turkey | cake | truck | grass |
| apple | bowl | hot dog | man |
| duck | snow | tiger | window |
| toy | egg | train | tree |

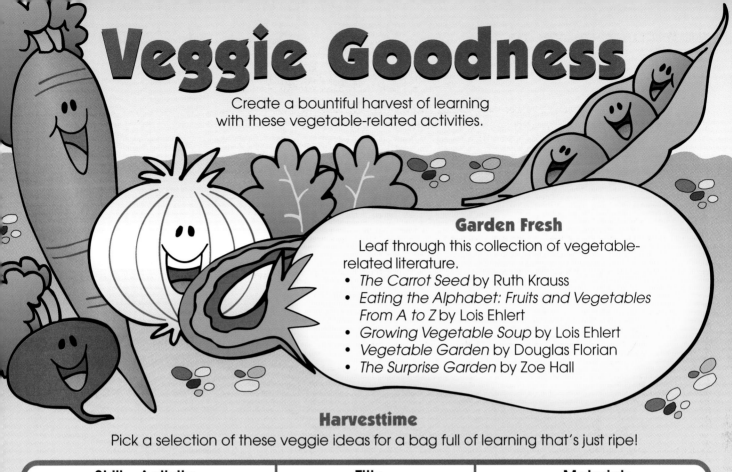

# Veggie Goodness

Create a bountiful harvest of learning
with these vegetable-related activities.

## Garden Fresh

Leaf through this collection of vegetable-related literature.
- *The Carrot Seed* by Ruth Krauss
- *Eating the Alphabet: Fruits and Vegetables From A to Z* by Lois Ehlert
- *Growing Vegetable Soup* by Lois Ehlert
- *Vegetable Garden* by Douglas Florian
- *The Surprise Garden* by Zoe Hall

## Harvesttime

Pick a selection of these veggie ideas for a bag full of learning that's just ripe!

| Skill—Activity | Title | Materials |
|---|---|---|
| Writing words—puzzle, list | "Mixed Veggies" | white construction paper copy of page 176, 9" x 12" sheet of colored construction paper |
| Observation, recording—booklet | "Window Garden" | copy of page 177, two 2¾" x 3¼" sheets of white paper, 3 green bean seeds, resealable plastic bag with a paper towel stapled inside it as shown |
| Vocabulary, matching—game | "Veggie Batch Match" | white construction paper copy of page 178 |
| Vocabulary, writing a list—song | "Eat Your Veggies" | copy of the top of page 179 |
| Vocabulary—cooking | "Very Veggie Snack" | copy of the bottom of page 179 |

## Edible Extras

- Send home a note encouraging parents to have their child write (or draw) a grocery list that includes vegetables. Then invite them to let him help with grocery shopping and preparing a vegetable for a meal.
- Include a simple graph as shown. Invite each child to survey family and friends at home to determine the favorite vegetable of the group. Then suggest that the graph be displayed on the refrigerator and used to help plan meals.

Veggies!

peas  carrots  corn  broccoli

# Mixed Veggies

**Parent note:** Carrots and broccoli and peas—oh my! This puzzle is great for the veggie lover in your family. Have your child remove the construction paper from the bag. Help your child cut out the puzzle pieces and then assemble and glue the puzzle onto the construction paper. (For a more challenging activity, ask your child to cut each piece in half before assembling the puzzle.) After the glue dries, assist your child in coloring and labeling each vegetable, then creating a list of five more vegetables on the back of the paper. If desired, display the finished puzzle on your refrigerator as a reminder to eat plenty of healthy veggies.

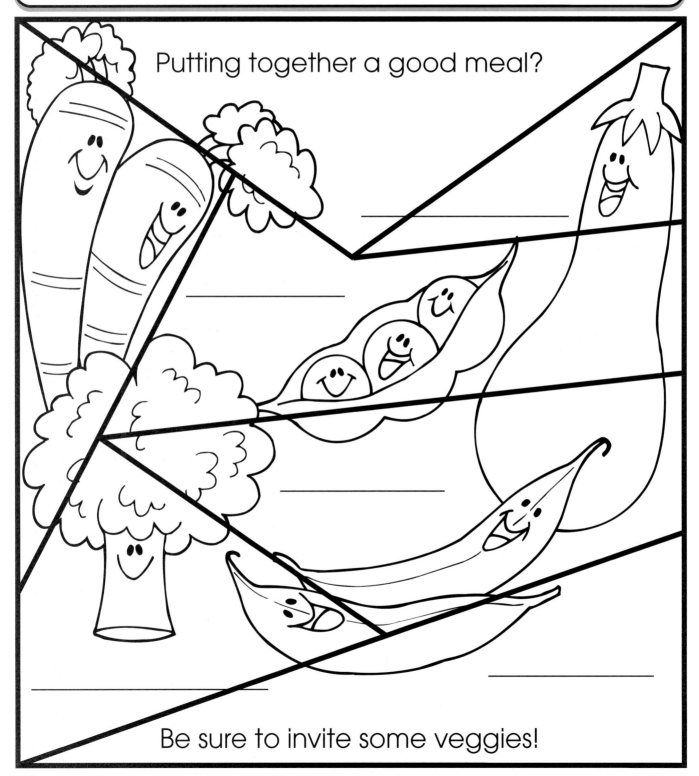

Putting together a good meal?

Be sure to invite some veggies!

# Window Garden

**Parent note:** This teeny-weeny bean garden is perfect for little hands! Have your child remove the blank paper, resealable plastic bag, and seeds from the bag. Assist your child in cutting apart the pages below and the cover at the right and stacking them in order. Next, help him or her place the blank paper behind the other pages and then staple them to make a booklet. Help your child read and follow the directions below to set up and observe the experiment.

## Directions:

1. Read pages 1–3.
   Follow the directions to set up the experiment.
2. Check the bag each day.
   Watch for the seeds to sprout.
3. Draw the plants in your booklet.
   Write about them.
4. Wait two days.
   Look, draw, and write again.

The sprout is bigger.

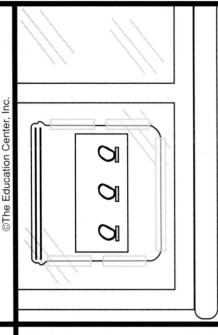

_____'s seeds sprout!

(Name)

©The Education Center, Inc.

**3**

Tape the bag to a sunny window.

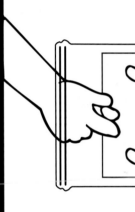

Plant three seeds.
Seal the bag.

**2**

**1**

Pour in water.

©The Education Center, Inc. • *It's in the Bag!* • TEC4100

177

# Veggie Batch Match

**Parent note:** One potato, two potato—match! Have your child color and cut apart the cards, turn them facedown, and give half to a partner. Next, help your child read and follow the directions below to play this domino-style game. For some extra letter and sound practice, have your child point out letters he or she recognizes and then say the sounds.

## Directions:

1. Pick up your top card.
   Lay it faceup.
   Read the words.
2. Your partner picks her top card.
   She reads the words.
   If a word matches, she places it next to the matching word on the other card.
   If no words match, she puts it back in her stack.
3. Take turns picking and matching cards to those that have been played.
4. The first player to use all his or her cards wins.

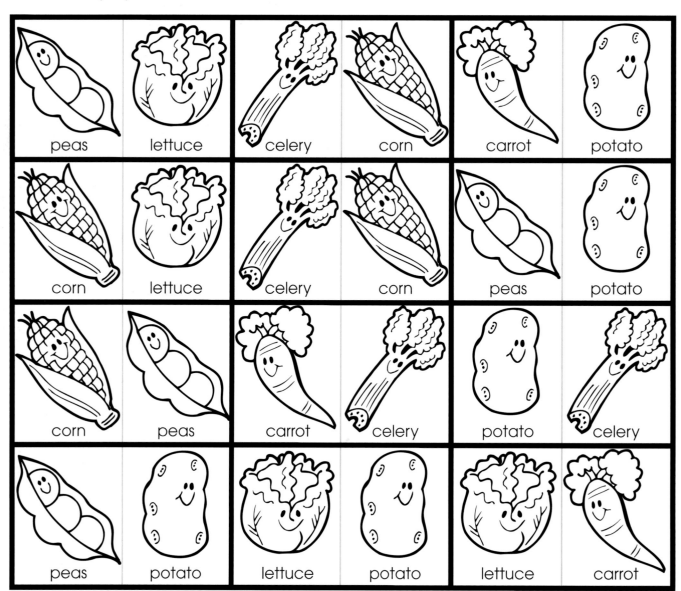

# Eat Your Veggies

**Parent note:** This little ditty is fun to sing with your child as you're making a grocery list or planning meals together. On the back of this sheet, brainstorm a list of vegetables with your youngster. Then help your child read and sing the song below. Encourage your child to repeat the song, each time substituting the underlined veggies for new ones from the list.

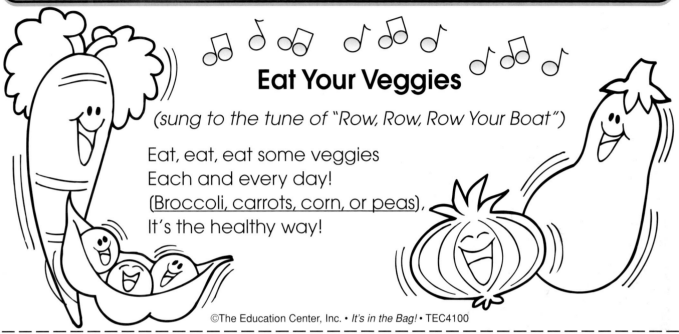

## Eat Your Veggies

*(sung to the tune of "Row, Row, Row Your Boat")*

Eat, eat, eat some veggies
Each and every day!
(<u>Broccoli, carrots, corn, or peas</u>),
It's the healthy way!

©The Education Center, Inc. • *It's in the Bag!* • TEC4100

---

# Very Veggie Snack

**Parent note:** Looking for a way to entice your youngster to eat a variety of vegetables? This funny-face snack is just the thing! Gather the ingredients; then wash and cut up the vegetables with your child. Help your child read and follow the directions below to make this healthy, fun treat.

**Utensils and supplies:**
plastic knife
small plate
tablespoon

**Ingredients:**
broccoli florets
cucumber slices
black olive slices
cherry tomatoes
red pepper slices
carrot slices
1 tbsp. ranch salad dressing

### Directions:

1. Put the dressing on the **plate.** Spread it out.
2. Pick some **vegetables.**
3. Use them to make a funny **face** on the plate.
4. **Eat** your snack.

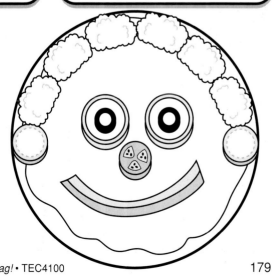

©The Education Center, Inc. • *It's in the Bag!* • TEC4100

# Wonderful Weather

Rain, snow, or shine, your students and their families will have wonderful weather-watching experiences with this unit.

### Forecast of Great Books

It's raining facts and fun with this supply of weather-related books.

- *The Cloud Book* by Tomie dePaola
- *Cloudy With a Chance of Meatballs* by Judi Barrett
- *It Looked Like Spilt Milk* by Charles G. Shaw
- *The Wind Blew* by Pat Hutchins
- *Flash, Crash, Rumble, and Roll* by Franklyn M. Branley

### It's Raining, It's Pouring…

…and nobody's snoring! Pack this weather bag to go, and skills will be strong in the morning!

| Skill—Activity | Title | Materials |
|---|---|---|
| Storytelling—story starters | "The Day It Rained…" | copy of page 181 |
| Collecting and recording information—journal | "My Weather Journal" | 2 copies of page 182 |
| Oral language—report | "Weather Reporter" | copy of page 183, photocopied map of the United States |
| Creative writing—craft | "Story in the Sky" | copy of page 184, 6–8 cotton balls, 9" x 12" sheet of blue construction paper |
| Vocabulary—mobile  | "Weather Reminder" | copy of page 185, paper plate (precut as shown), five 12" lengths of yarn |

### Extended Forecast

- Send home a note suggesting that each family watch a local weather forecast and then discuss the appropriate attire for the following day.
- Encourage each family to sketch or take photographs of various types of weather and then compile the pictures into a unique weather record book.

# The Day It Rained...

**Parent note:** This is a great activity to enjoy after reading *Cloudy With a Chance of Meatballs* by Judi Barrett. Talk about crazy, zany weather with your child; then help him or her read and follow the directions below. Enjoy telling several wacky weather stories with your child. If desired, tape-record your child telling the stories for a creative keepsake.

## Directions:

1. Cut out the raindrops.
2. Toss the raindrops in the air. Catch one.
3. Tell a story using the story starter on your raindrop.

The day it
rained pennies...

The day it
rained jelly beans...

The day it
rained flowers...

The day it
rained marshmallows...

The day it
rained sneakers...

# My Weather Journal

**Parent note:** So what's the weather currently like in your area? This journal activity will engage your child in reading and listening for information and then recording data. Each day, encourage your child to read the weather page in the newspaper, listen to a weather report on the radio, or watch a newscast weather report on television. Then have your child write to record weather information in the journal. If you have an outdoor thermometer, have your youngster check it daily and then record the temperature. Provide assistance as your child reads and follows the directions to make a weather journal. When the journal is complete, talk with your child about the weather changes over the four-day period.

## Directions:

1. Cut out the pages.
2. Stack them.
3. Staple the pages to make a journal.
4. Record weather data each day.

---

## My Weather Journal for

_____
(day)

Date: _____

Today we had
☐ sunshine
☐ rain
☐ wind
☐ snow
☐ fog
☐ other _____

The temperature was _____

I thought the weather today was _____ .

---

## My Weather Journal for

_____
(day)

Date: _____

Today we had
☐ sunshine
☐ rain
☐ wind
☐ snow
☐ fog
☐ other _____

The temperature was _____

I thought the weather today was _____ .

# Weather Reporter

**Parent note**: There will be blue skies in North Carolina today! Have your child remove the map from the bag; then study it together as you discuss current weather patterns in other parts of the country. Next, display the map at your child's height, and store a roll of tape nearby. Then help your child read and follow the directions below to practice giving a weather report.

### Directions:

1. Cut out the cards.
   Stack them.
2. Choose a card.
   Read the word.
3. Tape the card to the map.
4. Give a weather report.

| | | |
|---|---|---|
| sunny | rainy | snowy |
| windy | stormy | cloudy |
| cold | hot | warm |

# Story in the Sky

**Parent note:** After reading an imaginative book about clouds, such as *It Looked Like Spilt Milk*, spend some time with your child lying in the grass, looking up at the clouds. Encourage your youngster to search for animal or object formations in the clouds. Then go back inside and have your child remove the cotton balls and blue construction paper from the bag. Encourage your child to pull the cotton balls into interesting cloud shapes and then make a picture with them on the construction paper. When your child is satisfied with the cloud picture, invite him or her to glue it in place. Then help your child read the story starter below and write a creative story about the cloud in the sky.

It looked like a cloud in the sky. But it was really a....

# Weather Reminder

**Parent note:** What causes all the different types of weather? Reread a nonfiction book about weather; then help your child complete this mobile to keep track of how four main types of weather form and look. Have your child remove the paper plate cloud and yarn pieces from the bag. Next, help your child read and follow the directions below to complete the weather mobile. Then invite your child to hang the completed mobile in your home.

## Directions:

1. Color the pictures.
   Cut them out.
2. Read each description.
   Fill in the missing weather words.
3. Cut the descriptions out and match them with the pictures.
   Glue them together.
4. Tape one end of a piece of yarn to each picture.
   Tape the other end of each piece of yarn to the cloud.
5. Hang your mobile.

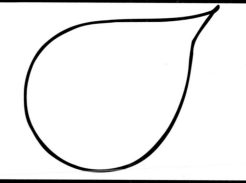

**Rain**
In a cloud, tiny water drops bump together and get bigger. When they get big, the drops fall as _____ .

**Wind**
The _____ moving around us is called wind.

**Snow**
Tiny bits of ice in clouds grow into big flakes. When the flakes get big, they fall as _____ .

**Thunder and Lightning**
Lightning is electricity leaving a storm cloud. After a _____ bolt strikes we hear_____ .

# Let's Go to the Zoo!

What could be more fun than a trip to the zoo? How about a bag full of activities made especially for you?

## Tour Guides

Give your youngsters a bird's-eye view of the zoo with this collection of animal-friendly books.
- *Good Night, Gorilla* by Peggy Rathmann
- *If I Ran the Zoo* by Dr. Seuss
- *My Visit to the Zoo* by Aliki
- *Polar Bear, Polar Bear, What Do You Hear?* by Bill Martin Jr.
- *Zoo-Looking* by Mem Fox

## "Zoo-ming" Off!

Pack your bag with the following assortment of activities and send your little ones on a zoo adventure they won't soon forget!

| Skill—Activity | Title | Materials |
| --- | --- | --- |
| Matching, oral language—activity | "Feed Me!" | copy of page 187 |
| Classification—diagram | "Where Do I Belong?" | copy of page 188, 12" x 18" sheet of construction paper with a Venn diagram labeled as shown |
| Creative writing—story starter | "My Day at the Zoo..." | copy of page 189 |
| Matching sentences and picture clues—cards | "All in a Day's Work" | copy of page 190 |
| Action words, oral language—mask | "Lion Tales" | copy of page 191, half a paper plate, craft stick |
| Reading, oral language—song | "Who's in the Zoo?" | copy of page 192 |

## Zoo Extras

- Extend your little ones' zoo adventure by including a note asking each child to write about his favorite zoo animal. Encourage him to share his writing with his family.
- Include a simple graph for each family to complete together. Ask each child to survey his family members and then graph each person's favorite zoo animal.

Skills: *Matching, oral language—activity*

# Feed Me!

**Parent note:** It's feeding time at the zoo, but the new zookeeper doesn't know what each animal likes to eat! Help your child read the clues at the right, solve each riddle, and then draw a line to match each animal with his dinner. Ask your child to explain his or her answers. That's a relief—these animals will sleep well tonight!

### Clues:

1. I like to peel my favorite snack.
   I eat it while lying on my back.

2. There is only one treat for me.
   It is green and grows on a tree.

3. I use my sharp teeth to eat my food.
   I growl when I am in a bad mood.

4. I have floppy ears shaped like a bell.
   My favorite snack comes in a shell.

# Where Do I Belong?

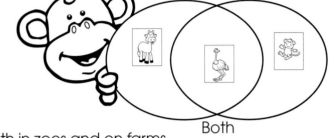

### Directions:

1. Color and cut apart the animal cards.

2. Sort the cards.
   Make one pile for farm animals.
   Make one pile for zoo animals.
   Make one pile for animals that can live both in zoos and on farms.

3. Glue the farm animal cards in the Farm section.
   Glue the zoo animal cards in the Zoo section.
   Glue the cards of animals that can live in both places in the Both section.

| kangaroo | ostrich | horse | monkey | elephant |
|---|---|---|---|---|
| zebra | sheep | pig | snake | chicken |
| lion | cow | giraffe | duck | goat |

# My Day at the Zoo...

**Parent note:** Talk with your child about what it might be like to visit a zoo. Or help your child remember a fun day at the zoo, and ask him or her what zoo animals were favored and why. Next, discuss with your child what may happen at the *beginning, middle,* and *end* of a zoo day. Then help your child read and follow the directions below.

**Directions:**

1. Draw your face on the child.

2. Write a story.
   Write about the beginning of a zoo day.
   Write about the middle of a zoo day.
   Write about the end of a zoo day.

3. Draw a picture for your story.

4. Read your story.

## My Day at the Zoo...

First,

Then

Finally,

Skill: *Matching sentences and picture clues—cards*

# All in a Day's Work

**Parent note:** What does a zookeeper do all day? Talk with your child about the important work a zookeeper does; then encourage your child to tell you what he or she sees in each picture below. Help your child read the sentences below and then cut them out. Have your child match each sentence with the correct picture and glue it in place. To finish the activity, help your child think of another part of the zookeeper's job, draw a picture of it in the last box, and write a sentence about it. Zookeepers sure are busy people!

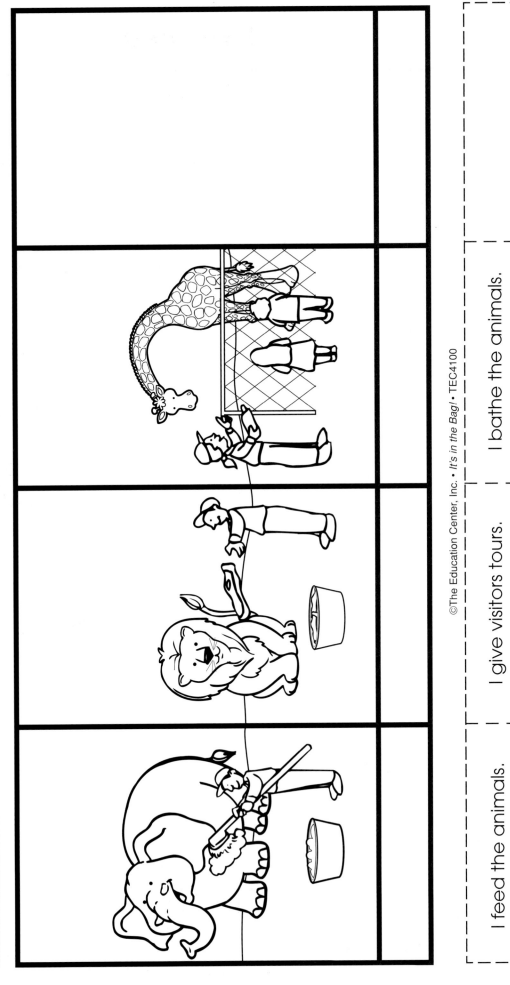

| I feed the animals. | I give visitors tours. | I bathe the animals. |

# Lion Tales

**Parent note:** Growl! Roar! Leap! Discuss with your child some of the possible actions a lion can perform. Next, have your child remove the paper plate half and craft stick from the bag. Help your child read and follow the directions below to create a lion mask. Tips: In Step 2, help your child cut out the eyeholes. In Step 4, help your child fringe only the outer rim of the plate. When the mask is complete, encourage each family member to use the mask and say the sentence in Step 9 aloud, completing it with an action word (*roar, leap, growl,* etc.).

## Directions:

1. Color the mask yellow.

2. Cut it out.
   Cut out the eyeholes.

3. Color the rim of the paper plate orange.

4. Cut fringe around the rim.
   Try not to cut into the middle of the plate.

5. Cut out the center of the plate.

6. Glue the mask onto the rim.

7. Tape on the stick.

8. Hold the mask up to your face.

9. Say the following sentence, filling in an action word.

*I am a lion, and I can _____!*

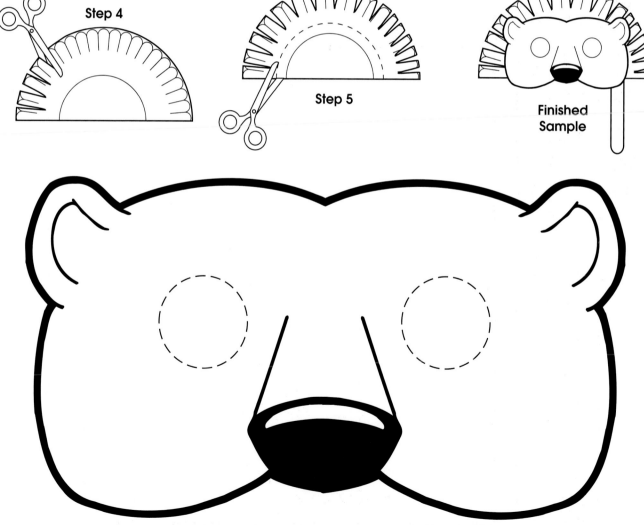

Step 4

Step 5

Finished Sample

# Who's in the Zoo?

**Parent note:** No visit to the zoo is complete without a song! Help your child read the song below; then sing it together. Next, help your child think of additional zoo animals, sounds, and actions to make up more verses. For even more zoo fun, encourage your child to act out each verse as it is sung.

### Who's in the Zoo?
*(sung to the tune of "The Farmer in the Dell")*

The monkey's in the zoo.
The monkey's in the zoo.
Eeek! Eeek! Hear him screech.
The monkey's in the zoo!

The lion's in the zoo.
The lion's in the zoo.
Roar! Roar! The crowd wants more.
The lion's in the zoo!

The bear is in the zoo.
The bear is in the zoo.
Growl! Growl! He's on the prowl.
The bear is in the zoo!